THE
DO-IT-YOURSELF
BUSINESS BOOK

THE
DO-IT-YOURSELF
BUSINESS BOOK

GUSTAV BERLE

WILEY

JOHN WILEY & SONS
New York • Chichester • Brisbane • Toronto • Singapore

ISBN 0-471-50768-7
ISBN 0-471-50769-5 (pbk)

Printed in the United States of America

10 9 8 7 6 5 4 3 2

ACKNOWLEDGMENTS

The author wishes to express gratitude to the innumerable sources that have helped to provide ideas and statistics, facts and figures, and especially encouragement.

Among the valued resources for factual material were the U.S. Small Business Administration, the U.S. Department of Commerce, the U.S. Department of Labor, and the U.S. Chamber of Commerce, whose director, Ivan C. Elmer, deserves special kudos.

Many among the 13,000 volunteers in SCORE, the Service Corps of Retired Executives, have been of inestimable assistance, in particular Executive Director John E. Daniels.

Fellow author Jeffrey P. Davidson and my literary agent, Bert Holtje, were of tremendous help and inspiration, as were John Wiley & Sons' senior editor Michael J. Hamilton, his assistant Marilyn Dibbs, and copyeditor Caroline Meline. To all of the above and all those I have failed to mention, a thousand THANKS.

GUSTAV BERLE

Washington, DC
June 1989

ABOUT THE AUTHOR

Gustav Berle was in turn Director of Marketing and Communications, as well as Director of Membership and Training, for SCORE, the Service Corps of Retired Executives. The largest volunteer, small-business-counseling organization in the world, SCORE has 13,000 volunteers working out of more than 750 locations in all 50 States. Through the end of 1988, more than 2,300,000 entrepreneurs and would-be entrepreneurs had sought SCORE's counsel in one-on-one sessions or workshops. Mr. Berle has participated in this organization both as a volunteer in the field and on staff in the national office in Washington. He also has been editor-publisher of small business trade magazines and has written numerous articles on various phases of entrepreneurship. He taught subjects related to this field for 18 years at the University of Baltimore.

CONTENTS

CONTENTS

CONTENTS

CONTENTS

CONTENTS

Part One

How to Prepare Yourself for the Right Business

INTRODUCTION

John Hancock once said, "The more people who own little businesses of their own, the safer our country will be and the better off its cities and towns. For the people who have a stake in their country and their communities are its best citizens." And today small business is the major bulwark of our national economy. Small business accounts for 98 percent of all business in this country and almost half of the jobs; 38 percent of the gross national product and 42 percent of all sales. Businesses with less than 100 employees create nearly two million jobs a year, with the greatest number coming from firms with less than 20 people. The American dream of starting your own business is as strong today as it was 200 years ago.

From *You Can Make a Difference,* a film made for SCORE, the Service Corps of Retired Executives Association.

THE DREAM OF INDEPENDENCE

The dream of some 600,000 Americans every year is to BYOB—Be Your Own Boss. Getting into a business of your own is not only an achievable dream, but a calculated risk that can lead to riches or ruin. This book is designed to give you a candid, easy-to-absorb overview of most of the problems you'll encounter *and* solutions—as well as to inspire you, stimulate you, and help you minimize the risks.

The realizable dream for so many entrepreneurs can be a home-based business; a garage enterprise; a small, family partnership; a formally organized corporation; or just a part-time, freelance, or consulting attempt at achieving some degree of independence and additional income.

Sadly, the majority of these businesses do not survive the first five years. Still, the picture is not as bleak as it is often described.

You can take out some "insurance" against failure and disappointment in a number of ways. Getting experience in your chosen field, amassing sufficient working capital, taking a realistic look at the market and your competition, selecting good counsel and abiding by it, and, above all, being knowledgeable about the realities of a business of your own—these are ingredients that can combine to spell $uccess.

Entrepreneurship Is In

This is a good time to contemplate starting a new business or acquiring an existing one. During most of the past decade academic institutions and our government have been playing catch-up with small business. Previously it was felt that national and international welfare was vested in the big corporations. Academic studies revolved around organizational structure, including lines of responsibility and authority, and the key management principles of planning, staffing, organizing, directing, and having control.

Gradually, the importance of small business has been realized by academic and governmental institutions. Initially, academic courses were few and far between and were offered as downsize versions developed for the larger corporations. Then we saw more courses emphasizing innovation, creativity, and "doing your own thing." Even large organizations paid attention to "intra-preneurship"—encouraged some of their creative executives to develop fast-track departments under the umbrella of Big Brother that were seemingly independent of the sponsor.

Labor statistics confirmed that small businesses exhibited faster growth than large corporations. Small entrepreneurs employed Americans at a sizably accelerated rate over corporate giants. Various government departments—the Small Business Administration (SBA), Commerce, Agriculture, Energy, Defense, and others—have been falling all over each other offering assistance to small entrepreneurs with advice, literature, seminars, and loans.

In the nation's erudite press, learned academicians who write on all phases of business, suddenly focused on entrepreneurship as a favored topic. Thirty-one percent of all articles in four leading journals of business and finance were devoted to this theme during the past two years.

This new surge of individualism and creativity has gone abroad, too.

Even in the USSR, that hotbed of anticapitalism and collectivism, *perestroika* has become pals with cautious entrepreneurship. The new Russian administration has succumbed to the simple logic that people work better when allowed to make their own mistakes and gather the fruits of their own efforts—that is, under the relative freedom of entrepreneurship.

Canada's Immigration Example

North of the border, Canada offers a more readily accessible example of entrepreneurship. According to the Canadian Federation of

Independent Business, located in Toronto, Canada is a world leader in the number of immigrants who open small businesses here. In an "Eleven Nations Study" undertaken by the CFIB's umbrella organization, the International Small Business Congress, a remarkable phenomenon was revealed.

With the 11 nations studied representing the globe, it was found that Canada experienced the greatest growth of small business in the world, and this was spearheaded by the country's large immigrant population. Immigrants now own more than 16 percent of the small businesses across Canada. By way of comparison, the average ownership by immigrants of small companies in industrial nations is only 8 percent; in developing countries, 7 percent—half the Canadian figures. A more benevolent immigration policy has been responsible for stoking the Canadian economy, and Canada has thus become the world leader in channeling new entrepreneurial energy into economic gain.

Crossing back into the United States, the nationwide trend is toward small-business expansion, in the formation of both independent small businesses and feeder companies that attract and support larger corporations. Said Doug McAllister, director of the SBA's Northern Florida office, "More and more people are leaving major corporations to form their own small businesses. Entrepreneurship is the buzzword."

THE ENTREPRENEUR: WHAT MAKES HIM OR HER TICK?

1

ADDICTED TO FREEDOM

Entrepreneurs are a mystery to some people, especially those who are only comfortable with a nine-to-five existence and assured weekly paychecks and fringe benefits. The entrepreneur is a business person who prefers to take calculated risks in order to be his or her own boss. To the entrepreneur, BYOB does not mean "Bring Your Own Bottle" but "Be Your Own Boss."

Sometimes the entrepreneur is regarded as a business person who takes risks. This is not so. An entrepreneur is a business person who *minimizes* risks. He or she does this by advance planning, research, and meticulous consideration of all factors that could affect and possibly endanger his or her enterprise. When the entrepreneur forgets to do advance investigation and preparation, then he or she is a gambler at best, and a failure statistic at worst.

A few short years ago the *CPA Client Bulletin*, a newsletter not known for casual opinions, wrote about entrepreneurs as follows: "It has been said over and over again: the small American entrepreneur is something else. When the economy was in a tailspin, with interests way up in the double digits and bankruptcies being racked up faster than during the great depression, what was the hard-pressed small operator doing? Picking himself up, brushing off the dust and starting a new business!"

The newsletter then cited figures to prove that more than 600,000 new businesses were incorporated in a single year in the United States, and said that "While we were shaking our heads over all those bankruptcies a year or two ago, we should have known the little guys and gals who were going through the ringer weren't out of it for good. Many of them weren't even ready to go to work for somebody else. They had tasted independence and would settle for nothing less. So what if they flunked out last time? This time would be different. The great unbossed. There's nobody like them."

The newsletter writer's insight gets to the heart of the true entrepreneur. Even Frank Sinatra expressed it in one of his popular songs: he picks himself up and starts all over again. The genuine entrepreneur looks at catastrophe as the fertilizer for the next growth.

Says Professor Karl Vesper of the University of Washington, "Businesses continue to be launched by people who didn't make it the first time around. A driving force in entrepreneurship . . . is addictiveness. Once people have a taste of freedom in a business of their own, they like it. They don't want to go back to working for someone else."

There are other factors to note about the acceleration of entrepreneurship: (1) Growing numbers of retirees, especially those who have moved to the Sunbelt, start up small businesses of their own—often having nothing to do with their former livelihoods. (2) Those who have been laid off due to plant relocation, corporate mergers, or bankruptcies seek solace and security in business enterprises of their own. (3) More and more workers are joined by their spouses in the formation of small businesses. (4) The vast increase in service industries and technologically assisted businesses makes independence more feasible. (5) Deregulation allows small entrepreneurs to set up businesses, often acting as "feeder industries" or contractors to larger enterprises that were formerly their employers.

WOMEN ENTREPRENEURS

Enter: the woman entrepreneur. A quiet revolution has materialized during the past half-dozen years that "promises to have a resounding impact on the economy in [this] decade," according to Charlotte Taylor, a Washington business consultant and former President Carter's Women-Business-Owners task-force coordinator.

While the percentage of growth for men entering into business independence could be measured in the teens, women's increase in a single decade was 69 percent.

Counselors for SCORE, the Service Corps of Retired Executives that advises hundreds of thousands of tyro business people each year, have noted that at least half, and often more than half, of their clients are women.

There is no mystery here. Women go into business for the same reason men do—to make money and to be their own bosses. The rise in female entrepreneurship is reminiscent of what the early-20th-century immigrants did—and the more recent waves of immigrants from the Asian trouble zones, Lebanon, and even Russia. When these future Americans arrived on American shores they, like today's American women, saw entrepreneurship as the fast track to success. Rather than take low-wage, big-industry jobs, they opted to use their wits and energy to climb the ladder of independence the entrepreneurial way.

THE ENTREPRENEURIAL PSYCHE

The national magazine *Venture* attempted to dissect entrepreneurs and to see what makes them tick. They conducted a survey to which 2,740 readers responded. Here is what they had in common: 1) Typically they were firstborn children who had a positive relationship with their father. (2) They held jobs before they were 15 and started their first businesses by the time they reached 20. (3) They borrowed money to launch their enterprises and made themselves personally liable. (4) Most of them are college graduates, consider themselves demanding of others, and start work early in the day (82 percent start work before 9 A.M.). (5) Twenty percent described themselves as successful; another 53 percent claimed moderate success; 27 percent reported the expectation of success.

While these entrepreneurs are intrepid adventurers on the business sea, they still seek the approval of others—often after they have launched an action. Respondent Richard M. Ask, president of the 2000-member National Association of Entrepreneurs, wrote, "I go out and do what I damn well please, and then I look around for approval to reinforce the action."

THE WHEN, WHEREWITHAL, AND WHICH
OF ENTREPRENEURSHIP

How old are the people who start new businesses? The majority are 30 to 34, with the biggest segment (70 percent) between 25 and 44.

Age of Entrepreneur*	%
Under 20 years	1
20 to 24	8
25–29	17
30–34	21
35–39	18
40–44	15
45–49	9
50–59	10
60 and over	1

* U.S. Small Business Administration

With what do entrepreneurs start up new businesses? How much money do they invest? Most businesses require between $20,000 and $50,000 in cash. The vast majority of business start-ups (87 percent) are in the range of a few thousand dollars to $100,000.

Start-Up Capital*	%
Under $5,000	17
$5,000–$10,000	14
$10,000–$20,000	16
$20,000–$50,000	25
$50,000–$100,000	15
$100,000–$250,000	8
$250,000–$500,000	2
Over $500,000	1

* U.S. Small Business Administration

Which businesses are the most popular? There is no doubt that retailing is number one. Nearly half of all new business start-ups are retail shops. Here is the line-up:

Type of Business*	%
Retailing	46
Services	19
Construction	8
Manufacturing	8
Finance	5
Professional	5
Wholesale	4
Transportation	2
Agriculture	2
Others	1

* U.S. Small Business Administration

WHAT'S YOUR E.Q.? TAKE YOUR ENTREPRENEURIAL QUOTIENT TEST

Here's how you can find out *before you spend any money* whether you've got the right stuff to become an entrepreneur!

1. It's good to be an OPTIMIST in starting a new business. If you think you are one, give yourself 4 points.
2. Personalities that go into businesses of their own are restless types, quickly bored with repetitive tasks. If you are like this, give yourself 4 points.
3. Strangely, many successful entrepreneurs are children of immigrant families. Are you? If so, give yourself 4 points.
4. You needn't have been an A student or a Phi Beta Kappa to become a successful entrepreneur. If you were just average, NOT an A student, give yourself 8 points.

5. Entrepreneurial types were often self-contained as teen-agers—did not join in teams and group activities too much. If you were that way in high school or college, add 4 points.

6. The same goes for your very young years. If you preferred to be alone when you were a youngster, give yourself another 4 points.

7. During these early school years, the entrepreneurial spirit shows up. Did you engage in any kind of business? News-paper route? Store work after hours? Baby sitting? Were you elected an officer in school? If any of these apply, you deserve another 4 points.

8. Determination as a child—usually referred to as stub-bornness—also counts. If you had this quality, give yourself 4 more points.

9. Were you and are you good at handling money? Did you man-age on what you had while at school? Such skill deserves another 4 points.

10. Writing things down is important to define goals. If you usually write down your considerations, take another 4 points.

11. A certain degree of caution is valuable. Taking calculated risks is OK, but being "a gambler" is not. Still, entrepreneurs are basically risk-takers. They venture frequently into un-chartered territory. If you did, and still do, you deserve 8 points.

12. If, despite their advice, you pursue different paths from your more conservative brethren, you should take another 4 points.

13. Boring daily routines are not for true entrepreneurs. Getting caught in a rut is often the motivator that propels an entre-preneur into business. If this is happening to you, or has happened to you, give yourself 4 points.

14. If you were a bank loan officer, would you think that entre-preneurs are too risky? If you wouldn't, you've earned 4 points.

15. Suppose your new business failed. Would you pick yourself up and start another business right away? If you've got that kind of determination, take 8 points.

16. Getting started is often tough and may require long hours, even all night. Would you be willing to work as long as it takes? If so, you get another 8 points.

17. Usually a single project is not enough for gung ho entrepreneurs. When they finish one project, they're ready to tackle another. Would you do that? If so, take 4 points.

18. Financing a new business is always risky. Assuming you have faith in your idea and your ability, would you risk your own savings? If you're positive, take 4 points.

19. Would you be willing to convince others and borrow from them, too? Yes? Take 4 more points.

20. If you have one or a dozen great ideas, do you go out and implement them immediately? Or are you more likely to research the market, the product or service, the competition, the financing, make a business plan—and then forge ahead? Such pragmatism deserves at least 8 points.

Now . . . what's *your* E.Q.? If you scored on all 20 questions and made 100 points, you will indubitably be a successful entrepreneur. Barring unforeseen events in your family or problems with your health, or acts of God, you will have an excellent chance to "make it big"! If any of these questions were answered negatively, rethink your position, talents, product/service, and timing.

THE HUMAN SIDE OF ENTREPRENEURSHIP: LMPRSW

Even if you have scored well on the Entrepreneurial Quotient Test, don't resign or tell the boss to go to blazes. What you should do now is take inventory of the most important ingredient in your new business—YOU. "Forewarned is forearmed" has never been truer than in this case.

The YOU-checklist goes like this: LMPRSW. These letters stand for the following:

Loneliness. As the one-line saying goes, it sometimes gets lonely at the top. YOU are the boss and there might not be anyone else to turn to. Of course, you can talk to the mirror—but you'd better be careful you don't magnify your successes, or blow up your mistakes out of proportion.

Management. Some aspects of being the one responsible for the operation of your own business might be distasteful: negotiating contracts and leases; hiring and, yes, firing employees; applying for a short-term loan; exchanging goods or rectifying an employee's error; dealing with a difficult customer. These are some of the toughies you can count on, because they are predictable.

Pervasiveness. When you worked for somebody else, five o'clock might have been the end of the day. You went home and forgot about the hassles. It is doubtful that you will be able to stop thinking about your own business at the end of the working day. Being your own boss is a way of life.

Riskiness. Going into business is a gamble, no doubt about it. The better you prepare yourself for it, the more you reduce the risk. The worst scenario could be losing the business that you've worked so hard to build up. That is a trauma that would affect your lifestyle, your social status, your reputation and self-esteem, your family's well-being and your peace of mind. Hopefully this will never happen.

Status. As an employee, teacher, or military officer, you are enjoying a status that has been acquired over many years by many people. When you chuck that image and start a business, the built-in status is erased and you must start to build it anew, on your own. Some of the previous perks, like invitations to parties or paid travel, and fringe benefits such as insurance coverage and club memberships, are no more—until you replace them selectively as you can afford them yourself.

Working conditions. If you were with a large corporation or bureau before, you might have had a company car, a plush office, secretarial help, and paid benefits. These conditions are not usually available in your own fledgling business. You have to balance such luxuries with the size of your bank account and the necessity of once more "crawling before you walk."

Well, now you know. Still raring to go? Then by all means GO!

ENTREPRENEURIAL QUOTATIONS

The entrepreneur will take what seems from the outside to be a wild risk. But his high self-esteem means that it does not seem such a wild risk to him. Because he believes in himself so much, he calculates the odds differently.
Lyle Spencer, Business consultant

———

No matter how many problems you take off the back of a human (entrepreneur), that person will take on a new load equal to the relief.
Albert Shapero, Teacher and author

———

. . . executives in large corporations need to be right only 55 to 60 percent of the time to be regarded as successful. The entrepreneur running his/her own show cannot afford to be right such a low percentage of the time, and instead must be close to 90 to 95 percent.

> Jeffrey P. Davidson, author of *Avoiding Pitfalls of Starting Your Own Business*

. . . the road to successful entrepreneurship is still pitted with innumerable sinkholes that swallow up the great majority of new ventures, no matter how they started. Those who do have a good chance to succeed have these positive aspects going for them: . . . a determination to prepare beforehand, a beginning knowledge of basic management practices, and . . . knowledge of the business selected.

> Louis Mucciolo, "Starting Up," *USAIR Magazine*, July 1988

The most important characteristic a business person should possess is perseverance. The most important characteristic of the business itself should be quality and service.

> Erick Schonstedt, Industrialist

SIX STATEMENTS OF PERSONAL BUSINESS PHILOSOPHY

1. Your business will wait while you do someone a good deed. But the opportunity to do good might not wait while you attend to your business.

2. Time is a far more precious commodity than money. If the latter is spent or even wasted, you can recoup it. If you waste your time, it will be gone forever.

3. The knowledge of running your business successfully is a wonderful asset, but it must not be taken for wisdom. Running a business successfully is making a living; being wise is making a life.

4. True entrepreneurs know that they must be careful about being too careful.

5. Entrepreneurs are optimists. They never for a moment believe they cannot do the impossible. They disdain those who believe that the world is against them, for the latter usually discover that if they believe it, it will be so.

6. If you finally decide that you will go into business, then you are strong enough to live up to your convictions. For those who do, there are no obstacles, no precedents.

BEFORE YOU START $\boxed{2}$

TWENTY-POINT LIST TO EXPLORE READINESS

1. *Evaluating Yourself.* The 20-item Entrepreneurial Quotient (E.Q.) Test in the preceding chapter told you how to determine your suitability for entrepreneurship. If you took this test honestly (*you* graded yourself!), you got fuel for your enthusiasm—or learned a truth that can save thousands of dollars.

2. *Ask the Right Questions.* Do a little personal market research. The information librarian, people already in the business, accountants, lawyers, business consultants, professors, specialists, the nearest SCORE counselors, articles in trade publications, books on the subject, the articles "morgue" at your local library are all resources you need to consult before you take the big leap into independence.

3. *Crystal-balling.* Forecasting the future for the business you want to enter is a very difficult and chancy task—even for those

already in operation. However, the information you gather in your personal market research will give you a basis for it. Projecting trends, budgets, expenses, and growth are vital steps toward preparing a realistic business plan and ensuring that you are on the right track.

4. *Location.* Unless you are starting out in your garage or spare bedroom, the physical location requires detailed and careful study. (See Chapter 4.) Foot- and vehicle-traffic count, accessibility by common carrier, proximity to resources, nearness of competition, growth potential of the area, ethnic composition, condition of properties, prestige of address, cost per square foot in comparison with other locations, closeness to banks and post office, even convenience to your own domicile are just some of the considerations to be taken into account.

5. *The Business Plan.* This is your own guidepost. It will mark you as a pro in the eyes of others, especially your banker or other lender. Without it you are walking through the woods without a compass. Get some help from your accountant or a local SCORE business counselor and take time to make your plan completely and correctly—especially if you will be applying for a loan. In the latter case, don't leave home without it.

6. *Financing.* Accurate and realistic determination of your financial needs is the most frequently sought factor for entry-level small businesspeople. However, money, while a vital factor, is not the total answer. It is tied in with the preparation of a credible business plan, which you must have in order to talk to a banker or the SBA about a business loan. The more you borrow, the harder you have to work to pay it back—plus interest. If you take in a venture or regular partner in order to get enough money, you will have to share a large part of your potential income.

7. *Legal Considerations.* Study the pros and cons of different types of legal organization. Consider contracts, employment

agreements, and zoning and other permits. Talk to SCORE or a business lawyer and accountant *before*, not afterward.

8. *Business Organization.* How will you organize your business other than its legal setup? What office space will you have? Where? Hours of operation? What name is best—generic, personal, product identification? What about packaging, pricing, delivery, and shipping? What signs do you need? Stationery and forms? Telephones and other instruments of communication? Supplies and licenses, office equipment and storage needs, vehicles and parking, files and cash handling, etc., etc. Check and double-check, and be sure to keep track of costs and expenditures.

9. *Advertising.* It's necessary to let your potential trade know about your new business. Which media will you choose? Which medium or media will deliver the most coverage for your money? How much will it all cost? Do you have the money for it? Who will make up the ads for you and/or write good sales letters? Realistic evaluation is essential. It is often necessary to say NO to hard-sell solicitors. You can check circulation and costs of media yourself in many cases through the Standard Rate and Data Service, available in most major libraries.

10. *Public Relations.* Often you can get free "advertising" in the form of publicity for your opening and for your new product or service, or unique approach. When you place an advertising order, also explore possibilities for free publicity. In addition, building an image through attractive displays and signage, logo and vehicles, stationery and wrapping, needs to be part of your new business development.

11. *Supplies.* Opening a new business is like moving into your first home. You tend to load up with everything as if there's a never-ending shortage. Even if you have established credit at the local stationery store, go easy on charging. Sooner or later, you'll have to pay and that pile of start-up cash has a way of shrinking

like the proverbial violet. Check prices at the local variety store, chain store, or even supermarket. Some common supplies can be much cheaper, even in small quantities, at the mass-market stores.

12. *Bookkeeping*. Some people love it, some people hate it. Either way, you've got to have it. There is no way to run a business, repay loans, satisfy the tax collector, and pay your bills without accurate financial records. More than that, you need to have periodic financial statements that tell you where you're going, whether you're making any profit or just fooling yourself, and what aspect of your business needs more attention. If you don't have the expertise yourself to set up a credible, understandable system, get a good bookkeeper—even if it's only one day a week—to set up your books and keep them, your invoices, and checks in accurate and up-to-date order.

13. *Accounting*. It's like bookkeeping, only more sophisticated. As your business grows, the accountant becomes necessary to make sure that your records are kept accurately, your taxes and government reports are filed promptly, and periodic financial statements are prepared that will tell you whether you are making it or flunking.

14. *Operating the Business*. Whether you plan to establish a 300-square-foot kiosk or a 30,000-square-foot supermarket, you have to set some policies by which to run your business. Take these items for starters: Will you deal with cash or credit? How will you control quality? What about hiring and training personnel, storing supplies and merchandise, packaging and delivery, securing against inside and outside theft, physical maintenance, etc.?

15. *Selling*. Will you be selling at retail over the counter? Selling wholesale by delivery? Using self-service? Selling by mail order or telephone? Somewhere along the line, even as a professional, you will have to sell your products or services. You have to decide

how to do it, who will do it, if you're going to train others to do it your way, and, of course, how to pay for these services.

16. *Personnel.* Right at the beginning, even when you might be able to run your new business by yourself, your plan should include a way to expand. You can do that only with other people—salaried, commissioned, or profit-sharing personnel. Where will you find them? How will you train them? How will you compensate them? What fringe benefits will be desired? How will you motivate them? Dismiss them?

17. *Insurance.* You need to consider how you can protect your premises, your merchandise or inventory, your employees, your rolling stock, and even the continuity of your business if disaster strikes (natural or human or financial). A good insurance agent can advise, evaluate and guide you through this maze.

18. *Self-inventory.* To take stock means not only of your supplies and merchandise, but of YOU. Judge yourself candidly and without hype or bombast. Controlling merchandise and supplies is vital, too, but not as important as safeguarding your health and happiness. Take stock, because even though you're an entrepreneur, you're not a machine. All work and no play could make for dull work and management indeed.

19. *Personal Pitfalls.* Be candid about this and examine your character. The temptations to overspend or fudge are every-where—through expense accounts, cash in the till or checkbook, costly cars and entertainment, keeping up with the Joneses, taking items out of inventory, or using employees for personal chores. Lean on those more experienced and seek advice on personal business conduct ahead of time, not when the auctioneer comes.

20. *Emulate Success.* They are everywhere—your peers who have made it. Look them up; read about them; talk to them; emulate them.

TWENTY WORKSHOPS/SEMINARS THAT COULD BE USEFUL IN BUSINESS START-UPS

The business pages of many major newspapers carry announcements of seminars and workshops available to you throughout the year. They may be conducted by private promoters, local colleges, stock brokerages, and authors of business books. There are also those sponsored by government and quasi-government entities such as the Small Business Development Corporation (SBDC) and SCORE, which might cost only $5 to $25.

What should you look for before you spend your time and money on a two- to six-hour session? The majority of such workshops, especially those conducted by the Small-Business-Administration-affiliated organizations, speak generally to the subject of "how to go into business." But there are also more specific offerings. The following list of topics is typical of workshops that are being conducted or have been conducted by SCORE, the Service Corps of Retired Executives. You can watch for these in your local paper or call the SCORE or SBDC office listed in the blue section of your telephone book under Small Business Administration.

1. What is SCORE (or SBDC), and what can it do for you?
2. Should YOU go into business?
3. Is there a need for your product or service?
4. Single ownership, partnership, or corporation?
5. The business plan: why and how?
6. The right location and how to find it
7. What's the competition?
8. What are your product/service advantages?
9. How to market: packaging, advertising, promoting, public relations
10. Legal and accounting problems: patents, trademarks, taxes

11. Help: how to get it, train it, keep it, reward it
12. Financing: research and development, start-ups, the first year
13. Zoning and licensing problems
14. Networking: trade associations, professional associations, service/civic memberships, seminars, trade shows, international trade
15. Continuity: how to keep it going; avoiding the conflicts of family corporations
16. Franchising pros and cons, leasing versus ownership, starting versus buying a business
17. Pricing your products and services for survival and profit
18. Computers and how to use them
19. Brainstorming and networking
20. Consulting after the workshop

TEN UNIVERSITY PROGRAMS THAT OFFER ADVANCED BUSINESS TRAINING

For those readers who have their sights set on doing business according to Hoyle, and who already have an undergraduate degree, the following alphabetically arranged list of 10 top business programs (selected from among many others) might be a useful guide:

1. Babson College's Center for Entrepreneurial Studies, Babson College, Wellesley, MA 02157-0907, (617) 239-4448
2. Harvard's Management Program, Graduate School of Business, Harvard University, Glass Hall, Boston, MA 02163, (617) 495-6450
3. Louisiana State University's Executive Program, College of Business Administration, LSU, CEBA 3139, Baton Rouge, LA 70803, (504) 388-8455

4. Northeastern's Executive Development Program, Center for Management Development, Northeastern University, 236 Huntington Ave., Boston, MA 02115, (617) 437-3272

5. Stanford University's Executive Program for Small Companies, Graduate School of Business, Stanford University, Stanford, CA 94305-5015, (415) 723-3342

6. University of Pennsylvania's Snider Entrepreneurial Center, The Wharton School, U of P, Steinberg-Dietrich Hall, Suite 3200, Philadelphia, PA 19104-6374, (215) 898-4856

7. University of Southern California's Entrepreneur Program, Graduate School of Business Administration, USC, Los Angeles, CA 90089-1421, (213) 743-2098

8. University of Southern California's Graduate School of Business Administration, USC, Los Angeles, CA 90089-1421, (213) 743-0034

9. University of Virginia's McIntire Entrepreneurial Executive Institute, McIntire School of Commerce, UVa, Monroe Hall, Charlottesville, VA 22903, (804) 924-3218

10. Wichita State University's Center for Entrepreneurship, WSU, Campus Box 147, Wichita, KS 67208, (316) 689-3000

AVOIDING PITFALLS

3

To be successful as an entrepreneur, you have to build a company around your whole life, not just the business aspect. You have to figure out what's really important for you and your family, and then you have to run the business accordingly. Otherwise you're going to have some very unhappy people around as the business grows. I think that's one of the reasons so many people who start companies don't succeed.

Warren Rodgers, computer entrepreneur

TWELVE COMMON SMALL BUSINESS PITFALLS AND WHAT TO DO TO CORRECT THEM!

PITFALL 1

Lack of experience: It is vital that the start-up entrepreneur know his or her product or

What to do about it: Recognize and analyze your limitations. Perhaps you need to call in an

service—how to buy or make the product, how to attract customers, how to handle finances, and how to train and manage others. It's great to be a specialist, but it's even better to be a business person with a balanced variety of experiences. Experience should be obtained, if at all possible, both in easy and hard times.

outside specialist or consultant; perhaps you should take a special course or even get a short-term job to learn the hands-on solutions. Consider a partnership with a person who has the skill you lack.

PITFALL 2

Lack of planning: Sudden ideas fanned by naive enthusiasm sometimes pass for inspiration. It is good to be motivated, of course, but drifting into business without a solid plan is like sailing in uncharted waters without a compass.

What to do about it: The more you rely on others in your business (suppliers, employees, managers) the more you need a plan of operation. Pre-opening market research of every facet of the business can dispel uncertainties and prevent later losses.

PITFALL 3

Lack of record keeping: Many people going into business detest the nitty-gritty keeping track of purchases, sales, expenses, losses, and taxes. By not knowing where you are going, you can fool yourself into problems with

What to do about it: Prior to opening any business, take a basic course in bookkeeping or accounting, or one on how to deal professionally with the person you engage. Keep good records for as long as the IRS demands them; keep

customers and the tax collectors, or even bankruptcy.

synopses for as long as you plan to remain in business.

PITFALL 4

Not knowing the balance sheet: This will tell you about the fiscal health of your business. Learn how to read and analyze it. The balance sheet makes sure you don't fool yourself into business suicide. Pay particular attention to liabilities. They are monolithic and will remain no matter what your assets.

What to do about it: Make sure your debts are paid promptly. Watch your working capital to see the trend in net-worth retention of profits. Ask your accountant or bookkeeper to explain the figures on your balance sheet if you don't quite understand them. It's your lifeline!

PITFALL 5

Leaping before you look: In the heat and enthusiasm of getting started, we tend to overlook probable consequences. Look before you leap is never truer than in starting a business. Ask questions, read up on everything published on the subject, check the competition, do your market research first; act afterwards.

What to do about it: Make a list of questions, then set out to gather the answers. Keep digging until you succeed. The answers you don't have before you make a commitment can cost you dearly later. A consultant, SCORE member, friendly competitor, even your librarian could have the information.

PITFALL 6

Insufficient use of suppliers: Once you're in business, the people you buy from, whether

What to do about it: On this list, include your banker. A line of credit can be among your

goods or services, want to see you succeed. Don't overlook them in seeking solutions to business problems.

greatest future assets. Talk things over with your manufacturer or wholesaler. They have seen problems similar to yours, and often they will "stake" you to longer terms or special buys.

PITFALL 7

Ignorance: There is no worse businessperson than the one who says, "Don't confuse me with the facts. I know all about it!" In any enterprise, education is a lifelong occupation. Only Adam was the Indispensable Man; you and I have much to learn yet.

What to do about it: Attend business clinics at the local college; go to meetings with people in your line of business; join professional and trade associations; read trade publications; use local library facilities, and check out government information resources, all as part of your entrepreneurial education.

PITFALL 8

Not seeking professional advice: Outside pros have experiences that can cut your losses before they occur—chances are that they have made mistakes and paid for them. Not talking to them makes it likely that you will make those mistakes, too—whether you make them with your own or somebody else's money.

What to do about it: Ask around for recommendations and find the right professionals to guide you to a proper start. Ask questions. Also ask how much this advice costs. Make sure to include such costs in your start-up financial projections.

PITFALL 9

Isolation: The saying "no man is an island" is ever so true for entrepreneurs. Don't be so secretive that you secrete yourself right out of business before you even get started. Don't feel you're the only genius in this world or that others are jealous of your aspiration. You might discover that some, not all, of your fellow citizens will be very happy to help you. It might make them feel good, too!

What to do about it: There are two broad categories of assistance you can call on, and for the most part they are FREE. One is networking with friends, peers and kindred organizations. You'll be surprised at how many people enjoy helping you and how much hidden knowledge they have to pass on to you. The other source of free information is the government—local, state, and federal. The SBA, Department of Commerce, SCORE, and private-sector organizations like the Chamber of Commerce are founts of welcome information. (See Part III)

PITFALL 10

A superman complex: Watch your health. Small business is very dependent on the vigor and well-being of its guiding spirit—YOU—at the same time that it is very demanding. It will require more than the usual hours; it can sap your energy and

What to do about it: Before you seriously engage in a demanding business, make sure that your health—both physical and emotional—is in tiptop shape. Ensure support from your family. Resolve any personal and financial problems first, so that you can

strength if things go wrong. It can affect your relationship with your family.
Entrepreneurs are subject to financial pressures that were not encountered when Friday was payday; and they are prone to "burn out."

concentrate on the big problems. Plan periodic relaxation and vacations to renew mind and body. These should be part of the planned overhead.

PITFALL 11

Uninformed employees: In a very real sense, your employees are your partners in progress. Informed and motivated employees can be your best assets. Their stake in the financial success of the business directly affects their efforts, and one of the most common drains on profits is through indifference by employees or internal theft.

What to do about it: Plan early in your business career to meet with your employees on a regular basis. Let them know what's going on and why. Make their workplace comfortable and humane. Plan to have a suggestion box; give ready access to your office; include fringe benefits such as health protection and profit sharing after they have been with you a while.

PITFALL 12

Ignoring customers: Since the customer is the focus of your business, it stands to reason that the customer requires primary attention. And when you figure out what it costs to attract and sell a customer,

What to do about it: Talk to your customers whenever you can. Assign someone in your company to spearhead customer relations, if you don't do it yourself. Make sure all employees, from clerk

then keeping that customer becomes doubly important.

to deliveryperson, know the customer's importance and their dependence on the customer. Sell user benefits in everything you do in your business.

FIFTEEN REASONS WHY BUSINESSPEOPLE FAIL

Many reasons are put forward about entrepreneurial failure. While we do not want to dwell on negatives, we'll make this list concise and to the point.

1. *Lack of Experience.* This is the number one culprit, as indicated in the 12-point list above. Don't let your own enthusiasm get in the way of reality. Business failure is a steep price to pay for I-strain. If need be, get a job in the field of your interest for a limited amount of time. Keep your ears and eyes open and learn all you can about it. Even if the money you make is not what you think you're worth, it will be cheaper to earn less for a limited time than to lose your own hard-earned savings and others' investments because of inexperience.

2. *Lack of Capital.* The second most important cause can usually be cured by realizing that it always takes more money to start a business than you think it will, simply because it takes longer to reach success than you had anticipated. Prepare a sound, thorough, rational business plan that tells all about you and your future aspirations, because only with such a plan will you be able to get enough investment money or an adequate bank loan or line of credit to see you through the known and unknown obstacles of the new business.

3. *Poor Location.* While this factor applies primarily to retail establishments, distributors and manufacturers also must weigh

the need for accessible locations; favorable traffic patterns; truck, rail, and sea shipping facilities; and proximity to labor markets, equipment, supplies, and raw materials. Retailers must be careful to clock traffic by vehicle and foot and investigate the proximity of public transportation and competitive enterprises, the social and ethnic structure of the neighborhood, and even future changes in road patterns and zoning.

4. *Inventory.* The wrong kind or too much of anything, especially in the wrong season, can sink the business. Inventory means money tied up. Get to know the normal turnover needed in order to make a profit in your kind of business. A friendly competitor or trade association should be able to tell you.

5. *Permanent Equipment.* Knowing how much to acquire, how to keep it working at optimum capacity, how to maintain it in peak condition, and how best to finance its cost are all factors that can lead to success or cause failure.

6. *Poor Credit Practices.* Selling merchandise or service on credit beyond your capacity to finance it can sink you. From the beginning, arrange to have charge-card operations, banks, or credit institutions take over the financing of sales. The few percent it costs is cheaper than borrowing more capital.

7. *Personal Expenses.* Take out only what you can replace through earnings or don't need for business operations. Many small, new businesses have failed due to the "pink Cadillac" syndrome or trying to "keep up with the Joneses."

8. *Premature Expansion.* Ambition can be a terrible burden. Before you make plans to expand your premises or your capital equipment, personnel, merchandise lines, etc., seek advice from an experienced counselor or banker, and customers. Make sure the extra business is there to pay for the expansion—and then double the estimated time it will take to achieve your plan.

9. *Bad Attitude.* Ignoring the complaints of customers, suppliers, and employees can lead to an even worse malady—they can start to ignore you. If you find yourself resentful of the very people on whom you depend for a living, then it's time to take a vacation. Maybe for good.

10. *Too Many Expenses.* Every business has a certain ratio to determine what it can pay for expenses such as rent, personnel, insurance, and advertising. Your accountant can advise you; your trade association will know. It's up to you to control each facet, adjusting it to reality. Discipline yourself to conduct your business within its means.

11. *Poor Collections.* If you extend credit too generously or fail to invoice and collect promptly, you can run out of the capital you need to operate your business properly. Then you will have to borrow more money at high interest rates or factor your receivables at an even higher cost.

12. *Low Sales.* This cause is fundamental. Loss of sales due to competitive reasons, style changes, inadequate sales efforts, changes in road patterns, etc. is the chief business malaise. Big sales cover a multitude of sins, but creating the better mousetrap is also one of the hardest jobs in the world.

13. *Inventory Mismanagement.* It's not enough to have the right inventory; equally important is to keep track of it, store and restock it properly, have it insured, protect it from damage and theft, and avoid its obsolescence.

14. *Competition.* Even if there is no competition in the immediate market area initially, success will soon attract competition. Have you ever tossed a piece of bread to a hungry sea gull or pigeon? Within seconds dozens of other birds come flocking to the scene to fight over every crumb. Preparing for such competition through proper pricing, display, service, selection, and promotion is a basic commandment of running business.

15. *Crime.* Cases have been recorded in which embezzlement or internal thievery has put a small business out of business. Analysis of your physical operation, warehousing, and storage for security, and attendance to bonding and insurance requirements are needed if you wish to survive the regrettable dishonesty of our real world.

TEN WAYS TO AVOID HOME BUSINESS PITFALLS AND MAKE SURE YOURS SUCCEEDS

If you plan to start a kitchen-table company, or are fixing up the garage or basement for that new at-home business, you should be aware of some pitfalls. One thing you don't want is to become a failure statistic. Unfortunately, most of the tens of thousands of small businesses that cease operation after a year or two are home-based businesses. Of course, many of these domesticated entrepreneurs make more trips to the refrigerator than to the bank, or they find that the baby is in disagreement with mother's concentrated activity in the den, or that the new business interferes with the Wednesday-afternoon bridge club. But if you are serious about starting a small business in your home to save overhead during the early stages, you still will want to follow sound procedures. Attend carefully to the following points, and you will have a pretty good chance of survival and success.

1. *Don't Be a Stay-Inner.* Operating a business from home does not mean that you have to hibernate there. Going out once in a while is good for your business as well as your emotional well-being. You need to meet people, network your wares and ideas, and pick up new ones—find out what's going on out there. Look for breakfast and luncheon meetings of kindred individuals and organizations.

2. *Plan to Keep Good Records.* Just because you are the chief-cook-and-bottlewasher doesn't mean that you don't have to keep good records. YOU still need to know what you're doing, when, with whom, and for how much. Additionally, somebody else needs to know—your trusty tax collector. If you don't keep good records, sometime in the future you might trip yourself up. It doesn't have to be an elaborate system, but one that you can understand and that is complete and accurate.

3. *Time Is Money.* Your time is your stock-in-trade. Since no boss is going to pay your salary, you must regard the time you spend working, thinking, planning, researching, running out to make photocopies and buy stamps, etc. as a salable, and chargeable, commodity. Cost-account your own time, just as you would the work you might perform for somebody else. YOU are the boss. YOU pay yourself. And YOU better know what your time is worth.

4. *Avoid Buttinskies.* These are well-meaning friends and relatives who have been in the habit of popping in any time of day to chat or have a cup of coffee, or to drag you out shopping. No more. Now you are in business. Let them all know that you are serious about working, and set aside specific time, such as evenings, for socializing.

5. *Banish Bad Habits.* These time and efficiency robbers are hard to shake. What are they? Running to the fridge for a snack every hour; sleeping late; procrastinating less-than-exciting chores; making or taking a lot of personal calls; catching that afternoon soap opera on TV. You can probably think of a few others. Cut them out if you want to run a home business for profit.

6. *Set Up a Work Schedule.* Determine when you want to work and set up a schedule for yourself. This is especially important if you are in a business where people need to reach you by phone or in person. The schedule need not be absolutely rigid—after all, this would take some of the fun out of being in business—

but time for your income-gathering efforts must be reserved that you—and others—can count on.

7. *Create an Appropriate Physical Environment.* Being in business, even at home, is an admittedly serious and straining activity. You need to provide a decent environment for yourself. Dragging old desks and chairs from the basement doesn't add up to your ideal working environment. If you can afford decent furniture—comfortable work-chairs, good files—go for it.

8. *Let There Be Light.* Good lamps help to prevent eye strain. Ordinary household fixtures might not be adequate for working all day. Analyze your lighting needs carefully and don't stint on eye comfort; you only have one pair of eyes.

9. *Avoid Piles.* This point refers to paper: piles of magazines, newspapers, clippings, letters, books, invoices, correspondence, references. Discipline yourself to file away each day's accumulation, and it will be a small chore, indeed. Have enough file folders, labels, and cabinet space on hand—and a system through which to find the material again when you need it.

10. *Treasure Your Privacy.* Avoid making your bedroom your workroom, especially if you are married or sharing it with another person. Offices tend to get cluttered, and a bedroom is for privacy, relaxation, and resting.

A DOZEN TIPS FOR AVOIDING ENTREPRENEURIAL STRESS

1. *Set Realistic Goals.* Organize your time to set realistic goals and do first things first.

2. *Fix Your Focus.* Keep your mind on what is important and meaningful about your work.

3. *Share Responsibility*. Decide what is important for YOU to do, then delegate the rest. It'll get done.

4. *Uncork Your Problems*. Share your concerns with others and communicate with co-workers and employees.

5. *Support Network*. Socialize with other entrepreneurs to avoid isolation, loneliness, burn-out.

6. *Be Elastic*. If problems become too big for one person, revise your business plan or get a partner.

7. *Be a Columbus*. There is always more than one way of doing things; keep searching, explore.

8. *Learn to Let Go*. Escape to a personal hideway to get serious work done, and detach yourself when not working.

9. *Don't Sweat the Small Stuff*. Learn to relax, read a book, watch a movie, turn on a music tape, do a crossword.

10. *Do All Things in Moderation*. Avoid punishing your body, the only one you've got, with too much booze and rich food.

11. *Get a Move On*. That means do some exercise on a regular basis and try to make it fun-time when you do.

12. *Know Thyself*. Monitor your own physical and mental condition and maintain a healthy respect for your limits.

NUTS AND BOLTS CONSIDERATIONS 4

THE FORMAL STRUCTURE OF YOUR BUSINESS

There are three ways to organize your business formally. Each has pros and cons, and the choice is yours. If you have any doubt about how *you* feel comfortable with *your* business, talk to some friends who already are in business, or discuss this with a business attorney, accountant, or SCORE counselor. Even after you have decided on the kind of formal business structure that is right for you at this time, remember that legal entities are not engraved in stone. They can be changed in future years if your circumstances change. This overview will give you a quick comparison of your options.

The Sole Proprietorship

1. *Management Control.* You are to be in total control.

2. *Personnel*. Do you need other employees to complement and supplement your skills? And do you have the money to pay them?

3. *Continuity*. You need a plan in the event that you are unable to continue the business yourself. Who will carry on? How will your transfer such responsibility?

4. *Costs*. Little or no initial cash funding is needed.

5. *Capitalization*. If you need to borrow money, it will have to be on your own resources. Do you have them? Or do you have personal equity against which to borrow capital?

6. *Debts*. If anything goes wrong, you are solely responsible for losses. Can you afford that?

7. *Government Regulations*. These may include a license, local tax certificate, zoning certificate, and workmen's compensation number, if you plan to hire anyone.

8. *Taxes*. These can be handled through personal income tax filing, unless you have employees, who will need to file quarterly tax returns.

9. *Profits*. They all go to you, the owner.

10. *Growth*. It is limited by your own ability, profit reserve, and loan capacity at the bank.

The Partnership

1. *Management Control*. It is divided by two or more partners, unless an initial agreement is made to make one partner (generally the majority partner) the "managing partner." Limited partners are not part of actual management.

2. *Personnel*. Will the partners' skills be sufficient to run the business? Are your lines of responsibility clearly stated in advance agreements? If additional employees are needed, who will hire and train them?

3. *Continuity*. Do you have a survivor's rights agreement? How will any payout be handled and to whom? How are surviving family members of the deceased partner to be handled?

4. *Costs*. A general partnership agreement, which has fairly low legal costs, is recommended. Limited partnerships are more complicated, and responsibilities and liabilities of each need to be delineated clearly.

5. *Capitalization*. Have you clearly spelled out the amount of money each partner is to invest or contribute? How is this investment or contribution to be secured and repaid, if any payback is ever required? What interest or obligation is attached to such a fiscal contribution? How is the family protected in case of any default or death?

6. *Debts*. Partners are generally liable for all debts. Do you need a special agreement that sets forth limits in proportion to the investment? If you have limited partners, their liabilities are equally limited.

7. *Government Regulations*. These are similar to sole proprietorship; in addition, a partnership agreement should be drawn up.

8. *Taxes*. Partners pay their taxes as individuals.

9. *Profits*. They are divided among partners in proportion to their investment, or according to agreement.

10. *Growth*. It is limited by partners' skills and participation in the business, as well as by their individual loan capacity.

The Corporation

1. *Management*. The corporation acts as one entity, but the board of directors holds legal and formal control and votes in relation to number of shares held in the corporation. Working control is held by those who are in actual day-by-day management of the business.

2. *Personnel*. Management is more flexible; expert outside personnel are often hired.

3. *Continuity*. This form offers the most flexibility for transfer of ownership shares in case of departure or death.

4. *Costs*. These are higher than for the other business formations. Various legal forms, a charter, documents, and professional fees are all required.

5. *Capitalization*. The corporation provides greater loan potential through sale of stock and loans based on corporate financial strength.

6. *Debts*. The corporation is liable for debts only as a legal entity. Shareholders are liable only to the amount of their investments, unless they have given personal guarantees.

7. *Government Regulations*. Extensive record keeping is required, which differs from state to state. Corporations must have articles of incorporation, by-laws, minutes book, periodic meetings with financial reports, shareholders' meetings, tax and filing fees.

8. *Taxes*. Corporation pays tax on all profits. Shareholders pay personal tax on dividend income, which is actually double taxation on the same money.

9. *Profits*. They are divided among partners in proportion to their investment, or according to agreement.

10. *Growth*. This form offers the most flexibility. The board of directors can vote to retain any profit and reinvest it in future

growth, sell additional shares, or obtain loans on the corporation's credit or assets.

FINANCIAL CONSIDERATIONS

This is going to be a very vital part of your business plan. Just to make sure you have all financial needs accounted for, let's check off the different items that have to be included. You can divide your budgetary needs into two parts: start-up costs (which are usually nonrecurring, at least for some months or years), and monthly, or recurring, expenses.

Start-Up Costs

Rent and security deposits	$ ____
Utilities, installation and deposits	$ ____
Business vehicles, if any, including insurance, painting, signs	$ ____
Outside signs	$ ____
Interior decorating and fixturing	$ ____
Salaries or payments for training	$ ____
Equipment in office, shop, garage	$ ____
Licenses, permits, tax deposits	$ ____
Legal fees	$ ____
Accounting fees to set up books	$ ____
Starting inventory	$ ____
Initial insurance	$ ____
Interest on borrowed money for start-up	$ ____
Advertising and promotion for pre-opening and opening events	$ ____
Cash on hand	$ ____
Reserve for unforeseens	$ ____
TOTAL	$ ____

Monthly Expenses

Rent $ _____

Insurance on property, inventory, employees,
customers, management, vehicles, inside theft,
bonding $ _____

Salary (owner-manager) $ _____

Salaries (employees) $ _____

Fringe benefits, social security, workmen's
compensation, hospitalization, bonuses, incentive
payments, training and replacement costs $ _____

Telephone $ _____

Utilities $ _____

Office, store, and shop supplies $ _____

Taxes, social security, workmen's compensation $ _____

Interest on borrowed capital $ _____

Maintenance of property, vehicles $ _____

Professional fees, including legal, accounting,
advertising, public relations $ _____

Planned merchandise or inventory replacement $ _____

Vacation and absentee reserve $ _____

Professional business dues $ _____

Contributions $ _____

Advertising media costs $ _____

Postage $ _____

Subscriptions $ _____

Miscellaneous reserve $ _____

TOTAL $ _____

TWENTY-FIVE WAYS TO HELP YOU DETERMINE THE RIGHT SITE FOR YOUR BUSINESS

In the real estate business there is a truism:

Q. What are the three primary reasons for buying a piece of property?

A. (1) Location, (2) location, (3) location.

Keeping this in mind, here are 25 checklist items to help you be sure the site you select for your new business is worth the investment:

1. How is it located in relation to customers?
2. Are supplies, especially raw materials, readily available?
3. Is the labor market adequate and handy?
4. Is public transportation available to the place of business?
5. What is the road pattern that allows vehicular traffic or foot traffic to come to the new business?
6. If it is a retail business, what is the present traffic count? Pedestrian? Vehicular?
7. Is there parking in the immediate vicinity? If so, is it free or how much does it cost?
8. What are comparable pay scales for employees in the area?
9. Are there ethnic considerations that will affect the potential labor pool? What is the reputed work of this ethnic pool? Trainability?
10. Are there training facilities nearby, such as vocational schools, community colleges, universities, or specialized schools?
11. What are the availability and costs of utilities?
12. What is the local tax burden? Are there any incentive provisions during the start-up period? Reductions for hiring special employee groups?

13. How is the local business climate? Is the neighborhood generally receptive to your kind of business? Has there been a history favorable to it, or has the opposite been true (if you are occupying a previously operative business site)?

14. What possibilities exist for future expansion? Extra space should you need it? New roads coming in? Additional housing, schools or utilities planned?

15. If you are building, what is the actual topography like? Sloped? Flat? Type of soil? Drainage?

16. What is the municipal protection like? Police? Fire Department?

17. Is insurance readily and reasonably available? Do any reservations or restrictions exist?

18. Is there adequate and reasonable housing for employees?

19. Are there special environmental factors that you need to consider? Pollution?

20. What will this site be like in the future in terms of value? Access? Utility?

21. Where are your competitors located? Do they affect this location? If it is an industrial park or shopping mall, competition might be a magnet.

22. Is mortgage money readily available for this site? What is the banker's/mortgage company's opinion?

23. Is there any trade support from chambers of commerce or other useful trade groups?

24. What are existing media that could be useful for advertising and publicity? What are their rates?

25. Is there adequate storage/warehousing space at a price that makes sense? Or do you need cheaper warehousing facilities elsewhere?

A CHECKLIST FOR KEEPING BUSINESS RECORDS

There is no hard-and-fast rule as to how long you must keep business records. Often it depends on your space availability and your nostalgia. But since it is important, in fact vital, to keep some records, the accounting profession has suggested some guidelines, below. Your own attorney might advise you further, because some record retention depends on individual state statutes in addition to federal requirements.

Keep for Two Years

Requisitions

General correspondence

Keep for Three Years

Petty cash vouchers

Bank account reconciliations

Personnel files on former employees

Expired insurance policies that have no cash value

Keep for Six Years

Employee withholding tax statements

Employee disability benefit records

Monthly trial balances

Keep for Seven to Eight Years

All general canceled checks

Vouchers for payments to employees, vendors, etc.

Inventory records

Payroll records and time sheets

Payables ledger

Receivables ledger

Expired contracts and leases

Purchase orders

Invoices and other sales records

Operating cost ledgers

Keep Indefinitely

Audit reports and financial statements

Canceled checks for contracts, capital purchases, taxes

Cash books

Contracts and leases that are current

Copyrights, patent papers, trademark registrations

Corporate charter, minutes books, and bylaws

Correspondence pertaining to legal and tax matters

Deeds, easements, mortgages, property records

General ledgers and journals

Insurance records

Property appraisals

Stock and bond records

Tax returns and all supporting papers

BUYING A BUSINESS

5

TWENTY-FOUR-POINT QUESTIONNAIRE

Have you compared the total, realistic cost of starting a business on your own, with the cost of buying somebody else's business? Invariably the two are very close—in fact, starting a business might take less up-front cash, but it will ultimately cost more (however, most start-up entrepreneurs don't know this or won't admit it). If you're interested in buying an existing business, consider the following:

1. The most important question is, would YOU be comfortable and happy in this business?

2. Do you have the necessary temperament, education, skills, and experience to make this business successful?

3. Do you have enough money to buy AND operate this business AND have some left over in case things don't go quite as

you anticipate? Doing it on a wing and a prayer may be all right for stunt flyers, but not for those who are starting a business.

4. Do you intend to use the money you have set aside for operating and expanding this business? Or is it only for you to draw on while the business is developing? In the latter case, aren't you just buying yourself a job?

5. What are you actually buying? What physical assets? How much is for potential? How much is for "key money" or goodwill?

6. Sellers usually overestimate the goodwill. Since it is an intangible, is it subject to serious negotiation?

7. Is the business you are contemplating buying a highly personal one? Remember that customers usually buy the personal services of the owner and consider whether they can be transferred to you. How long will the owner spend with you to make sure?

8. Why is the owner selling the business in the first place?

9. If the business is losing money, is it because of bad management? (This can be corrected). Is it a bad product or service? (What makes you think you can reverse this fatal malady?) Is it a poor location? (That, too, is correctable.) Is there tough new competition? (This will take honest analysis and might be a warning that the market is oversaturated.)

10. If the business is losing money for personal reasons, is it because the owner is sick, or having marital problems? Is a relative-employee stealing him blind? Is the owner burnt out? Is he hiding real profits because he wants to minimize his taxable income?

11. Is it a situation where the business merely needs new capital, but the owner doesn't have it or know how to raise it? (This could be a real opportunity for a partnership or your takeover.)

12. Is the sale because of a business divorce? Partnership disagreements can break up a business and provide opportunities for outside acquisition.

13. Is it because of the death of an owner? This, too, can be a great opportunity, especially when the lawyer wants to settle the estate and get on with the probate. Sometimes the obituary columns are better leads than the "business for sale" classifieds.

14. Is the seller playing coy? If the person seems to be playing games or stalling for time, he or she might be hiding something you are not supposed to know. Don't waste your time on this turkey. Go to the next prospect.

15. Is this a business broker's bargain? The "business opportunities" columns are full of these magnets for the naive. They make interesting reading, but so do the comics.

16. If you haven't found the business you want to buy at a price you can afford to pay, have you made a "cold-call" mailing to existing businesses? Most good deals are not on the market. A sincere letter, a realistic offer, and credible proof of your sincerity and fiscal capability might dredge up some surprising results.

17. Have you used networking? Talking to sales reps, trade association executives, wholesalers and distributors, and competitors in an existing business can produce formerly unknown prospects.

18. Are there innovative methods of financing that could make the deal acceptable to both parties? You might provide for the old owner to retain some equity position that could be paid off over a specified period of time; take a "wrap-around" mortgage, in which the seller finances some or most of the sales price; or buy the business but not the accounts receivables.

19. Are you answering a "blind" box number or broker ad? If so, save yourself a lot of grief by having the advertiser respond

to a box number of your own or to a friend who will act as a screen.

20. Have you been able to look at three years, and preferably five years, of tax returns so that you can examine the business's past more credibly?

21. If the business you are planning to buy is an existing franchise, be doubly careful. Why is the current franchisee bailing out? Is it his or her own mismanagement, or is it the franchiser's inattention? Would you be better off to buy a franchise directly from the franchising company?

22. Who are your competitors in the business you're planning to buy? Domestic or foreign? What about location? Pricing? Reputation?

23. What is your forecast for the future of the business you are interested in? What is the product or service obsolescence rate? Is there foreign or out-of-area competition?

24. What resources does the projected business have that you can acquire? How solid are they? Can they be purchased on favorable terms? Are there any contractual obligations in your favor that will remain in force? Are there any hidden debts or relationships that might be good or bad for you? What about employees? They are one of the most important business "resources." Will they stay? What is their track record? What benefits do they get? When did they get their last raise?

THE CASH FLOW—SEVEN CRITERIA

The amount of money you need for living and operating a business in relation to the amount of money the new business can generate is the key formula in considering buying a business. Addressing the following seven points can give you the terms you need to fill in that formula.

1. *Balance Sheet*. What does the seller's balance sheet show for net profit or loss? Take into consideration that in a personally managed business, some fringe benefits or cash income are not always reported fully. In a "closely held" business, the reported and recorded cash flow needs to be scrutinized carefully.

2. *Owner's Salary*. This, too, needs to be evaluated with care. You might want to compare it to the salary you would pay a manager to run the business for you.

3. *Benefits*. This item is fairly open and individual. However, your estimates must be reasonable and stand the scrutiny of, let's say, a tax examiner. In this category figure reasonable amounts for automobile operation or allowance, travel, entertainment, insurance (personal, liability, fire and theft, health, even key-man insurance, bonding if any, income protection), and any other discretionary costs that need to be part of your operation of the business.

4. *Interest*. This item covers any business loan interest paid to the bank or to the private individuals. If you form a stock company that involves interest payments for preferred stock, that projected interest figure must also be taken into account. For example: You borrow $100,000. Of this sum, $50,000 will be in common stock and $50,000 will be in preferred stock on which investors receive a guaranteed 12 percent interest annually. This means that you need to budget $50,000 $\times$ .12 = $6,000 a year ($500 a month) for interest payments.

5. *Nonrecurring Expenses*. These are initial costs that are usually incurred when you start or take over a business. These expenses will not be repeated for several years, but must be accounted for in your initial projections. Included in this category might be legal expenses, setting up an accounting system of your own, changing

the outside sign, repainting trucks, taking inventory, advertising to announce the change, printing new stationery, etc.

6. *Noncash Expenses.* Depreciation of property, equipment, and inventory does not take money out of your pocket, but it nevertheless reduces the value of what you will be owning—and it should be considered in any valid projections.

7. *Equipment Replacements or Additions.* New brooms sweep clean, and such replacements or additions are realistic considerations. While this expense will be used in generating future cash flow, you still need to consider it up front.

UNFORESEEN EXPENSES

You don't know what these are but they had better be figured into your projections. This is not a matter of being pessimistic, but merely realistic. As a rule of thumb, many experts advise adding one-third more to your operating budget. To help you imagine unforeseen costs, consider the following potential occurrences:

1. Start-up expenses are more than you anticipated. It's hard to think of everything, even if you have had lots of experience and guidance.

2. You come across new equipment, furnishings, or merchandise that you hadn't known about but that will make a dandy addition to your new business. With a little nest egg set aside, you can make this unplanned expenditure.

3. The initial flow of clients or customers is much slower than you had expected. This diminishes your cash flow and draws on your cash reserves. Therefore, they had better be there.

4. Since business is a little slower than hoped for at the beginning of your takeover, you need more advertising and promotion. That costs money—usually up front.

5. As a new business owner, you may not have the same credit extensions from your supplier as the previous owner. If that is the case, or you want to do business with new suppliers, additional cash (or credit) will be required.

THE TWELVE-
SECTION
BUSINESS PLAN

6

THE HEART OF YOUR BUSINESS START

Central to all new businesses is the preparation of a business plan. It is what the blueprint is to the builder. Since the majority of start-up entrepreneurs need some amount of borrowed capital, the business plan is the key that can open the door to a money lender—whether that be a banker, a venture capitalist, or investors.

Of course, preparing such a plan can be a pain in the neck. If you get a good CPA to prepare one for you, figure that it can take the first $2000 or more of your working capital. If your lawyer does it, providing he or she has the experience, it could be twice that much. So wouldn't it pay to learn how to put one together?

After all, *you* are the one who knows more about the answers than anybody else. You have the dream, the vision for this new enterprise. You have done the research. You are going to develop it into reality and, hopefully, make it pay off.

It won't be simple or easy. But here, in one short chapter, is a thorough checklist of information you need to supply. Once you have these items on paper, you'll be ready for the loan officer or investor, but most of all you'll be prepared for . . . *yourself.*

CHECKLIST OF INFORMATION YOU MUST SUPPLY

I. Identification

1. Proposed business name
2. Business address
3. Actual business location with 9-digit zip code
4. Business telephone or temporary phone
5. Tax ID number and/or social security number
6. All principals who will be involved in the operation of your business, along with their mailing addresses, titles in the business, telephone numbers, and social security numbers
7. Your accountant, his or her firm name, mailing address, and business phone
8. Your attorney, his or her firm name, business address, and telephone
9. Your banker, bank name, branch, address, and phone
10. Your insurance agent, his or her company, mailing address, telephone, and kind of policies being carried
11. Your business consultant, if any, or anyone else who will influence the conduct and welfare of your business

II. Your Stationery

This is not a direct part of your business plan, but it is necessary for that professional look. Having a good letterhead with matching envelope, and perhaps even a business card, is like getting dressed with a jacket, dress shirt, and tie. It literally makes a statement. Initially, you might want to get just a few sheets of stationery, pending final approval of the loan and all the other ingredients that finally will put you into business. When you submit your business plan, it should be accompanied by a cover letter typed neatly on your new stationery. It might sound something like this:

Gentlemen (unless you know the name of a specific loan officer):

We are requesting a loan in the amount of $ _____ , for the purpose of _____ .
We would like the repayment to be spread over _____ years.
The source of repayment will be _____ . We are offering as collateral the following, having an approximate current value of $ _____ : _____
_____ .

Your consideration of this loan request is appreciated. Should further information be needed, please contact us at _____ .

Cordially,

(signature)

Name

encl. Business Plan

III. Purpose and Supporting Data

1. Describe the goals of the proposed new business.
2. If it is an existing business, state your reason for buying and expanding this particular business.
3. What experience do you have that will enable you to successfully manage this business? Make this a detailed résumé.

4. How much money will you need from all sources?

   a. Your own investment ＿＿＿＿＿
   b. Others' investment ＿＿＿＿＿
   c. How much you need to borrow ＿＿＿＿＿
   > TOTAL ＿＿＿＿＿

5. How do you plan to utilize these funds?
6. How will these expenditures benefit the business?
7. What terms can you realistically offer for the repayment of the loan?
8. What proof can you offer that you will be able to repay the loan on the terms that you stated?
9. What collateral can you offer? What proof of its current market value?
10. Who owns the above collateral? Or is it pledged?

IV. A Detailed Description of the Business

1. What is the legal description of the business (proprietorship, partnership, or corporation)?
2. If a corporation, in which state has it been or is it being incorporated?
3. Is this a regular corporation or a subchapter S corporation?
4. What classification of business is this (retail, wholesale, manufacturing, service)?
5. Is this a new business? Expansion of an existing one? Takeover of another's business?
6. What is your projected starting or opening date?
7. If this is an existing business, what is its history?
8. What is or will be the operating schedule of your business (months of operation, days, hours)?

9. Is this a seasonal or year-round business? If the latter, how will you operate the premises, personnel, stock, inventory?

10. Who are your suppliers? What will they be supplying?

11. Do you have or expect any credit? What are the terms?

12. What are the suppliers' quotes for merchandise or services?

13. Will they give you any technical help? Managerial assistance? Training?

14. What other assistance can you expect from other sources?

15. If the work you expect to sell is contracted out, who will the contractors be? What are their terms? Contracts? References?

16. If you are planning to build, remodel, or improve any premises on which you will do business, what are the specifications? Contractors? Costs? Terms? (Attach plans.)

17. What is so special about this business?

18. Why do you expect this business to be successful and profitable?

19. What research have you done to support your belief that this business will be a success?

20. What competition exists? Where?

V. Your Market

1. What is your primary audience—neighborhood, ethnic composition, age groups, sex, economic and social level, etc.?

2. What is the size of your market in terms of area and population?

3. How much of this market will you be able to sell or service?

4. Do you think this projected market has much growth potential? About how much?

5. If you think the market will grow, will you be able to share in this growth? How and why?

6.   How will you personally be able to meet the demands of this growing market?

7.   Will you have the money for this growth? How will you get it?

8.   How do you plan to price your products or services?

9.   Will you be able to make a fair profit with such prices?

10. Will you be price-competitive? Can you give some examples of your competition's prices?

11. How are you going to market (advertise and promote) your products or services?

12. What advertising media will you have available? Which do you plan to use, and what are their best costs?

13. Why are you going to pick these media?

14. Can you indicate what your advertising budget will be? What your timing (calendar) is going to be? Who will help you to prepare this advertising?

15. If servicing is going to be important, what ideas do you have to meet and beat your competition in this phase?

16. Will you offer credit? What kind?

17. What plans do you have for slow-paying customers?

18. If you plan to accept credit cards, which ones?

19. Attach any ideas for logo, slogans, ads, promotional items.

VI. Your Competition

1.   Who are your nearest competitors and where are they located?

2.   In what way will you be superior?

3.   Do you have any solid information on how your competitors are doing? What support can you give for your judgment?

4. Describe your competition in some detail. How are you different from your competitors? What are their evident strengths and weaknesses?

5. What have you been able to learn from observing them?

6. Do you know what "market share" they have earned?

7. How can you get some of that market share?

VII. Your Location

1. Why have you chosen this location?

2. Describe the neighborhood.

3. What zoning laws affect this location?

4. What other businesses are in this area?

5. Are any of them direct competition?

6. Did you consider other areas before settling on this one?

7. Why do you feel that this location is best for your business?

8. Is the rental cost compatible with your operation?

9. Will this location be fairly permanent or are you anticipating changes? If so, when?

10. Is the building you will be (or are) in owned by you, or leased?

11. If you have a lease, what are the terms, conditions, length, cost, taxes, escalator clause, percentage if any?

12. What are the physical features of the space or building? Enclose a copy of its floor plan.

13. Will you need to make any renovations? If so, do you have quotations or estimates from one or more contractors? Enclose them, too.

VIII. Management

This is perhaps the most important part. At least it will be to you. Here the business enterprise can rise or fall, for inept management is the single most frequent cause of business failure. Not only must the loan officer be satisfied with your answers, but most important of all, YOU must be satisfied with yourself and your candid answers.

1. Who are the principals of the new business? Give a detailed résumé of each.

2. Do you or any of the other principals have *related* business experience?

3. What are the proposed duties and job descriptions for each?

4. For each position listed, state the starting salaries or salary ranges. Include all fringe benefits.

5. Are there any outside management resources that you can draw on? Where are they located?

IX. Personnel

1. What are the positions for which you will have to hire people at the beginning? In the future?

2. Are these employees available? How will you find them?

3. What skills should these employees have?

4. What training will these employees require? How will you give them this training?

5. Can you make do with part-time employees? What schedules will they be working?

6. If you use full-time employees, will you have an overtime pay policy?

7. What wages will you pay? On what basis (weekly, hourly)?

8. What fringe benefits will you offer? What will these additional benefits cost?

9. Are any of the proposed employees family members?

10. Do you have any "succession" policy in case anything happens to you, or you decide to absent yourself?

X. Financial Information

1. If possible, supply a balance sheet—current if this is a new business, or for the past three years if this is an established business.

2. Do the same with an operating statement.

3. To the best of your ability, prepare a projection for your business—monthly for the first year, quarterly for the second year, annually for the third year.

4. Supply a projected cash flow on a month-to-month basis for your first year of operation.

5. Do the same with a break-even analysis.

6. What capital equipment will you need or do you already have? Make a list, complete with cost or value for each item.

7. If you have real estate, equipment, machinery, and vehicles in this business, supply appraisals for each—but check first to make sure the appraiser is approved by the bank.

8. Supply a financial statement for each individual who is a principal or cosigner or guarantor involved in any way with your loan application.

9. Attach personal tax returns, business tax returns, or any other documents that you think might be helpful in establishing the legitimacy or value of your business and collateral.

10. Are there any other assets you have or anticipate having that might be important to disclose?

XI. If You Are Buying a Business

Also see Chapter 5.

1. If you are buying somebody else's business, who started it and when?
2. Why is this business for sale? Be sure of the *real* reasons!
3. How was the purchase price determined? Is this customary in the industry? Was an appraiser or broker employed?
4. How much will you be paying for "good will" or "key money"?
5. Will the sellers take back any of the purchase price in the form of a loan? What are the terms?
6. What documentation do you have that indicates past trends of sales?
7. If one reason for selling is declining sales, why are they down? How will you counter this trend, or make other adjustments to absorb the decline?
8. What will you or your management do to make this takeover successful?
9. What, specifically, are you buying?
10. In analyzing the business that you are buying, attach details on the following items:

    a. Creditors who have sold merchandise and services to the business.
    b. Terms (cash, COD) on which they are sold.
    c. Value and age of inventory.
    d. Accounts receivables, including their age.
    e. Capital assets (machinery, fixtures), age, and condition.
    f. Debts of the business (will you be responsible for the liabilities?).

g. An appraisal of the above assets.

h. A comparison of values established by the appraisers with your estimated real values.

i. Photos of the business and location.

XII. Miscellaneous Checklist

___ The plat plan

___ Deed to the land

___ Blueprint or layout

___ Zoning permit or explanation

___ Property lease and options to renew

___ Building contracts

___ Business agreements (corporation or partnership papers)

___ Licenses and options to renew

___ Franchise agreements, if any

___ Management contracts

___ Maintenance agreements

___ List of major customers and terms by which you trade with them

___ List of principal suppliers and terms by which you trade with them

___ Credit cards accepted

___ Check approval system

___ Marketing literature: ads, promotional pieces, stationery, business cards, menus, sign reproductions, displays, etc.

___ Publicity articles

___ Annual report, if any

— Buy-and-sell or purchase-and-sell agreements
— Insurance carried (company, cost, coverage, agent, etc.)
— Waiver agreement with landlord (in case of default)
— Any other legal documents that are pertinent
— Patents and copyrights, if any exist

ONE HUNDRED WAYS TO PROMOTE YOUR BUSINESS

7

Ideas are a dime a dozen. It is the execution of them that makes them real. Still, every entrepreneur is also the source of a seemingly endless flow of ideas. Not all of them turn out to be practical. Sometimes only trial and error tells us which is realistic. But we can rely on the experiences of others—pinpointing some ideas that have been tested and used over and over again. If the entrepreneur ever runs short of ideas, there are two ways to replenish them quickly: through reading and research, and through brainstorming with other kindred spirits. It is amazing how, when the mind is open and receptive, new ideas (usually combinations and re-adaptations of several old ones) will appear. It is easiest to promote a retail business, because it is tangible, and the entrepreneur deals directly with the public. Services are a bit more intangible, and the positive results one expects are often more long-range and subtle. In manufacturing, the time frame between the promotional effort and the visible result is usually longer, and there are many "mister-in-betweens" to take into account. But any business can be promoted.

THREE PHASES

There are generally three broad phases to promoting a business: (1) advertising, (2) sales promotion, and (3) public relations.

Advertising is any promotional effort that is paid for and that utilizes a public, scheduled medium or vehicle. It is available to anybody who has the money to pay for it. Because it is a paid medium, it requires money (often a great deal of it) and must be budgeted by the entrepreneur in his or her forecast and business plan. The amount is usually a specific percentage of the expected sales of the product or service, although during the introduction of a new business or product, a lump sum may be allocated regardless of the percentage. Though advertising is a paid promotional function, it does not guarantee results. It is controllable only in that its content and timing are determinable.

Sales promotion is a broader function that includes everything except paid advertising. Unlike the in-store sales policies contained in the next chapter, it refers to all transient ideas that help to move merchandise or sell services, whether on one occasion or repeatedly. Sales promotion can include displays, signs and posters, direct mail, publicity (some companies relegate this function to public relations), packaging, sales incentives, contests, testimonials, imprinted novelties, painted outdoor displays on trucks and walls, cooperative promotions with other merchants or related product manufacturers, unique media such as painted balloons and roadside serial signs (remember Burma Shave?), and many more.

Public relations is corporate image building. Its function is to provide a favorable aura for you, your company, your products and services, and in this it can be quite subtle. Public relations includes keeping your delivery trucks attractive and clean, delivery people well groomed, stationery impressive, credit functions humane, employees primed for sales, product and service quality above reproach, telephone answering polite and informative, signage on your building clear and beautiful—and your name before your public at all times. The latter requires constant cultivation of local media and publicity outlets—newspapers, radio and TV stations, newsletters, bulletin boards, columnists, clubwomen, nonprofit organizations, and others.

If you want to carry out all these promotional activities yourself, fine, as long as you *do* it. If your mind is not constantly on these functions, you need to appoint an experienced employee to handle them, or hire, at a price you can afford, an outside agency who is interested in growing with you instead of milking you and then running away with the cream.

As a general stimulus, we are listing 100 ideas that can act as inspirational "starters," many of them hooked onto special events, which makes a promotional effort easier and more logical.

ONE HUNDRED IDEAS

Anniversary Promotion Ideas

1. Use the number of the anniversary in theme-related ways: a birthstone, flower, or wedding anniversary symbols can be tied to your business's promotion. Example: for a 25th anniversary—everything in silver.

2. Announce the cutting of a giant cake at a public ceremony, with pieces to be given out to those attending the "party."

3. Award something to every number customer corresponding to the anniversary year. Example: 25th anniversary—every 25th customer who walks in gets a prize.

4. Give a discount equal to the anniversary year. Example: 25th anniversary—give 25 percent off on selected merchandise.

5. Have a general prize drawing equal to the number of the anniversary. Example: 25th anniversary—offer 25 prizes awarded at the end of the event period.

6. Have prizes for customers born in the same year as the store. Example: 25th anniversary—every customer registering who is 25 years old currently can enter a drawing or be invited to a special party.

7. Have an exhibit of photos and memorabilia from the year the business was founded.

8. Announce two for one. Any customer who brings in a coin with date of the store's founding gets twice his/her money purchase.

9. Announce an anniversary price rollback. Feature specific items that were advertised during the opening year, *priced* as they were during the opening year.

10. Feature people who were customers during opening year. Requires advance preparation, photography, scheduling, and logistics in showing people's pictures in windows during promotions, as well as in ads. Good vehicle for local media coverage.

Bargain-Selling Ideas

11. If an item lends itself to mass display, pile it up the way grocery stores do oranges. Psychological tests have proven that mass displays sell more merchandise.

12. If you have a "slow mover," combine it as a package with a hot item and price them together.

13. Silent-auction selling allows customers to enter a "bid" for an item. At the end of the day the highest "bidder" is notified that he/she has "won" that item.

14. Encourage friends. Offer a substantial discount if the customer brings a friend who also buys that targeted item, both at a reduction.

15. Offer progressive reductions; each day the item is not sold, the price goes down a little. You can set a bottom price, and once it hits that level it will either go off sale or stay at the merchant's minimum price.

16. Offer a free item once several items have been sold—perhaps with a punch card indicating number of items previously purchased (good on small-ticket, repeat items such as hosiery, soap, coffee).

17. If you have a basement department or separate outlet store, shift "upstairs" merchandise to the "bargain" or outlet location at a reduced price. ("Savings go UP when you come down!")

18. Target one day a month, and the same day each month, to have odds and ends of merchandise specially tagged and marked down. It can become an institution that ultimately can lead to lower advertising costs and greater results.

19. Dollar days have been popular for a couple of generations. Merchandise can be sold for one dollar each, several items for a dollar total, or one item at a regular price and a companion item for one dollar.

20. Also popular are red tag days or red star days, in which certain items are specially marked and customers need to look for them. In the process, many regularly priced and ticketed items are sold.

Fashion Promotion Ideas

21. Devote one window to one main color, and have accessories in eye-catching colors to add drama.

22. Hold a fashion show in which members of a local women's society act as models. A percentage of all sales generated by the models' efforts is donated to their organization (and thus becomes a tax-deductible, charitable contribution).

23. Participate in county fairs or local shows attended by women, having your own models or members of a cooperating charitable organization wear your clothes. They can carry and hand out discreet invitations that entitle bearer to a discount when coming into the store. Models, in addition to basic pay, or contribution, get a percentage on any card returned for a discounted purchase.

24. A fashions-through-the-ages show can display styles worn since the founding of the store.

25. A fashions-and-luggage show can demonstrate how to pack fabrics that travel well, such as cotton blends and knits. You might cooperate with a local travel agency and/or luggage store to offer a prize of a trip and/or bags.

26. If you are near a college or university, contact all sororities and invite them to a special, back-to-books fashion showing. Discounts can be offered to be returned to the sorority for the maintenance of their house or a students' assistance program.

27. Hold a fashion show in which an appointed "board" of regular customers picks the fashions to be modeled and then sold at favorable prices.

28. Hold a "second breakfast," late-morning fashion show. One store reported that this show drew far larger attendance than afternoon events.

29. Take advantage of the local ethnic situation and have a show with the appropriate foreign-language commentator; take advantage of local weather conditions and have a show on ice, etc.

30. Coordinate fashion show with a local auto dealer, especially during the time when new-model cars are being introduced. Hold shows in both automobile dealership and store, transporting models in festooned cars (at least one or two convertibles, if possible).

Unique Advertising and Promotion Ideas

31. Run clearance ads in a classified ad format—dozens of small ads under specific categories. Different salespersons' names can be used to foster internal enthusiasm and participation.

32. For big-ticket items such as major appliances or cars, run individual classified ads with the salesperson's name and a telephone number other than the regular store number.

33. Check the year's calendar for sales days that fall on the 13th and run a "lucky sale" or a "baker's dozen" sale on that day. In 1990, for instance, 11 weekdays fall on the 13th, and two of them are on Fridays.

34. Sometimes humor can sell merchandise. Department stores in Buffalo and Baltimore each used a full-page ad headed "Cats and Dogs," with ad copy accompanied by light-hearted drawings. Both reported heavy traffic and repeated the page for several years at appropriate clearance times.

35. The backs of playing cards can be imprinted with the business's picture and name, then sold at or below cost. Each deck is 52 miniature billboards that last for years. If the store has a community room or restaurant, card parties can be held using these decks, which are then given to participants.

36. If you handle back-to-school merchandise, bookcovers imprinted with the store's name and art make good giveaways.

37. Shopping bags are one of the best and most visible store promotions, especially the better kind that get multiple use.

38. Have a good, glossy postcard produced with your store's or product's picture on it. The other side can have a facsimile handwritten message announcing an event, sale, customer days, discount, or just some news.

39. If your store relies heavily on salesclerks, the latter's input, enthusiasm, and participation in events can produce more sales than all the advertising in the world. Plan to use these internal "pushers" by offering prizes or special employee discounts.

40. Make good use of the local chamber of commerce by obtaining new members' names; do the same with your bank, newspaper routeman, and local movers or their agents—and send each new resident a welcome flyer with incentive to shop in your place of business.

41. Find out what your customers think. Set up a visible mail box, and invite customers to drop their suggestions into the box. Offer a suggestion-of-the-month prize (such as a $10 merchandise or service certificate).

42. Increase attention to store windows through games, such as guessing the price of an item on display, the number of coins in a bowl, the size of a certain garment, etc.

43. In a store where foods are sold or leisurely shopping is encouraged, have a fragrant coffee urn on at all times—whether to offer a cup of coffee, sell your own blend of coffee, or have customers linger (and shop) longer.

44. If yours is a women's store, establish an area for men only—which has appropriate magazines and daily newspaper available.

45. Have a mailing piece prepared for all good customers, datelined from a distant or foreign city (if it's a fine fashion store, Paris; if a diamond merchant, Amsterdam; if a travel agency, Mexico or other exotic destination)—letting them know that you

are there buying for them and will have the new merchandise available at a specific date.

46. Advertise a charities bazaar once a year to which you invite Girl Scouts (to sell cookies), women's groups which produce handiwork items and baked goods for sale, health-oriented organizations that offer blood-pressure testing, etc.

47. At graduation time, sponsor an in-store job fair where local industry representatives are invited to dispense information on their companies, as well as local business-help groups, noncompeting businesses, and service and civic clubs.

48. Quality is a buzzword that attracts a certain type of customer. Publish a list and description of the quality merchandise you carry.

49. "Personals" are very popular classified ads, especially the boy-looking-for-girl and personal-items-for-sale types. Offer a bulletin board where such items, listed on 3 × 5 cards provided for this purpose, may be displayed for one week free of charge.

50. Advertise via a "shopper's column," presenting a thumbnail illustration of merchandise with a 50–100-word description. Mention a store shopper by name, and show his or her picture.

Merchandising Ideas Up for Adoption

51. With the increase in popularity of flea markets, country fairs, outdoor auctions, sales sponsored by service and civic organizations, and other nontraditional merchandising events, stores can explore these as opportunities to move low-end, novelty, and discounted merchandise.

52. Multiple sales opportunities exist for many products. Sometimes all it takes is a little imagination: Slogans such as "if you care, keep a spare"; "share it with a friend"; "bring a friend

and share the savings" are ways of selling more of the same item without additional effort or expense.

53. Coordinate one item with another. This applies to fashion apparel as well as decorative and food merchandise. Show a scarf with a blouse or sweater, a tie with a dress shirt, socks with a pair of shoes, a belt with a pair of slacks, a wallet or credit card holder with a pocketbook.

54. Canvassing produces many prospects and occasionally results in extra sales. For example, go down a street when the sun is high and make a note of each house directly exposed to bright, hot sunlight. Each one is a prospect for awnings, sun shades, tinted-glass windows, double-glazed energy-saving windows, sunproof draperies. Look for signs of peeling paint on the exterior, and you have prospects for a painting contract. If the car in front of the house looks worn out, you've got a new- or used-car prospect. Ditto for lawn care and landscaping, outdoor illumination, security systems, driveway repaving, exterior door replacements, etc.

55. Visual aids long have been popular in schools; why not in shops? A travel agency can show a tape or film about cruises and exotic destinations; a book store can show films based upon books; specialty stores can present video demos on cooking, luggage packing, etc.

56. Taking trade-ins of merchandise is more of a psychological than a financial incentive. Offer cash discounts to men when they trade in old suits and coats, to householders when they trade in furniture and rugs, to women when they trade in an old fur for a new one. This approach stimulates customers to buy something new, and old merchandise can be sold in outlet stores or offered to charities for a tax deduction.

57. Personalization (monogramming) sells merchandise, especially gift items. This also ensures that the items will not be returned.

58. Merchandise featured in famous and influential magazines—especially fashions, jewelry, home furnishings, perfumes—can be shown along with the ad, mounted on your display under the heading "As Advertised in. . . ."

59. Employees can sell by example. Have your salespeople and executives on the floor reflect the up-to-date look of your merchandise by wearing some of the items, being familiar with them, and being able to discuss them with customers.

60. Weather influences sales. On a rainy day, be prepared to show raincoats, umbrellas, and overshoes. On a hot sunny day, put items that add coolness and comfort in the vision of the customer.

61. Events make for add-on merchandising. No one knows this better than the greeting-card companies who have messages for every occasion. Not all people have ideas on what they want to buy for holiday gifts. Offer timely displays and attractively printed lists of pertinent merchandise. Go over the calendar at the beginning of the year to PLAN such events prior to each holiday.

62. Seasonal activities are also subject to advance planning and merchandising. Camping, going back to school, seasonal sports (baseball, football, swimming, ice skating), gardening, picnicking, taking vacation trips, graduation and wedding time are all hooks on which to hang profitable merchandising techniques.

63. Liquidation of general small items can be achieved by adding a little risk and mystery to the transaction. If you sell a lot of popular small items that are in everyday use, package them in a "mystery bag" and let the sign do the selling: "Each Mystery Bag contains at least $2 worth of merchandise—it's yours for $1."

64. Book sales are becoming increasingly popular among public libraries. Likewise, book stores and book departments attract buyers by displaying hundreds of "remainder" books at low prices on

outside or special aisle tables. If you try this, divide books by price and/or category for easier browsing, and include a small selection at $1.

65. Do the same thing with records and tapes, but be sure all are sealed. To these you can add trade-in records at extra low prices.

66. Likewise, a busy sporting goods store can buy up used golf balls from the local club and then offer them in a mass display for a low price per dozen. If you have the appropriate apparatus, imprinting with customer's initial will spur sales.

67. Layaway is a merchandise method popular in some stores (especially in working-class neighborhoods). Post clear signs next to displays that tell the amounts of downpayment required and terms of on-going payments.

68. Mail-order competition is strong in some outlying and farm areas. If you carry merchandise comparable to items carried in a popular mail-order catalog, post the catalog page along with your price for the same merchandise. If yours is lower, you will make the sale. Check it out!

69. Demonstrations are great sales methods. In food stores and department stores, the suppliers often pay the demonstrator's fee. If the item to be demonstrated has an attractive aroma (like coffee or sautéed foods), it will waft over a wide area and draw people. Seriously consider this method for your next grand opening, anniversary promotion, or holiday introductions.

70. Health is an all-pervasive interest for more and more people today. If you have space and the kind of merchandise or services that could tie in with health concerns, consider the lease or acquisition of a good scale, blood pressure machine or other health-monitoring equipment. If an instrument is on a coin meter, you might want to provide coins or tokens to customers as an additional way of serving them.

Displays for More Sales

71. Some of the greatest window displays, in use since the 1940s, have been the stage sets in the Lord & Taylor Fifth Avenue (New York) store. The window dress can be lowered into the basement and trimmed like stage settings. At Christmas time especially, these windows, like the ones at Macy's, attract thousands of lookers—and, hopefully, in-store customers.

72. One store put a battery-operated gadget in the window that rotated and knocked on the inside of the window every few seconds with a small metal ball. It turned a lot of heads and got extra attention to the window display.

73. Color is a great eye attractor. Trimming windows in coordinated or monochromatic (all one color) format attracts viewers.

74. People seek information and prices. Store displays should have adequate signage that explains the item as a salesperson would. Unless the price would detract from the merchandise, a visible price will attract prospects instead of suspects.

75. Showing merchandise in use will enhance reception. Examples are a table set with a cloth, napkin, china, silverware, and fake food; a bed made up with sheets and blankets; a game set up instead of hidden in a box; appliances being used by mannequins; etc.

76. Sound, like color, attracts attention to a window or interior display. Look in any TV department and you'll see one or several TVs playing. Tapes, demo units, or automated noisemakers can be used in departments, whether to make sales pitches or simply to draw attention to that display.

77. Use "peepholes" to attract the curious, just like in the fence on a construction site. You can cover the display window with paper or "frost" and make holes at various levels so that

passersby are able to look into the window—and see the merchandise or messages you have displayed.

78. Themes can make for ingenious window displays. For instance, "You'll Jump for Joy When You Wear Our New Spring Fashions" might show a cutout or photo blowup of a kangaroo, surrounded by fashions; "Buying a Father's Day Present is No Puzzle at (Your Name)" might show a blowup of a typical dad, marked up like a jigsaw puzzle, surrounded by suggested gift merchandise.

79. Motion and movement attract attention and store traffic. Have a display on top of a mechanically rotating platform or étagère.

80. If items you sell are being advertised on TV, find out if slides or film strips are available that can be shown in the store in the pertinent department. This gets extra mileage out of the confidence that "nationally advertised" merchandise confers.

Cooperative Promotions

81. Joining with other merchants in the same area, street, mall or shopping center is more cost-effective for two reasons: (1) you can buy ads and promos cheaper in larger quantity, and (2) each participant acts as a magnet for the others, as customers enjoy greater selection and one-stop shopping.

82. As a specialty store, you can sell merchandise more effectively by coordinating your efforts with a nearby store that carries complementary merchandise. For example, a fashion merchant can borrow the shoes for a display, or the flowers or plants, or sporting goods, or vacation posters—all from merchants who receive due credit via signs.

83. The retailers in a small town set up an exchange bureau (this could be handled through the local chamber of commerce)

through which each member-merchant can process slow-moving merchandise that some other store might be able to sell. The plan has been operating successfully for two years.

84. A shopping center produced a bingo card game. Customers in every store were given cards. A special punch marked the participating store's square after any purchase in that store. When the customers had one "bingo row" completed, they could sign their names and addresses, deposit the cards in a central box, and thus be eligible for that weekend's drawing for a number of merchandise certificates or prizes.

85. Another center had hundreds of colorful, plastic eggs filled with candies, coins, or more valuable trinkets (such as costume rings). Each store displayed a basket filled with these eggs and a customer was invited to pick one after a purchase. Easter traffic was increased measurably.

86. Each member store of a mall had one mystery item in its window, marked with a special ID sign. Entry blanks were available in the stores. Customers had to go from store to store to find the mystery display item and enter its number/name on the entry form. Completed forms made customers eligible for that weekend's prize drawing. The promotion promoted store-to-store traffic.

87. While parking meters are a boon to the town treasury, they are a pain to purveyors of merchandise and services. In some communities, merchants collect dues to pay for one day's parking meter income; then they advertise that parking is free on that special sale day. In-store traffic invariably increases.

88. Exchanges are costly. One merchant offered a 5 percent discount if customer allowed the sales check to be stamped "nonreturnable."

89. County fairs are usually held out of town and draw customers away from the town center. In one community, the merchants got together to promote a county fair that utilized displays

around the town square and along the main street—keeping customers in town, where merchants set up outside tables and displays.

90. One town, an agricultural center, did a lot of its business on Saturday nights. During the week merchants offered tickets to the local movie theater—good only on Saturday night—at greatly reduced prices. It brought hundreds of country folks to town to get tickets during the week and again on Saturday night. Many stores stayed open after the movies to do extra business.

Credit and Collection Ideas

91. Flattery will get you somewhere! One store has a pleasant-voiced lady call past-due accounts and say the store received a check that was unsigned—and wondered if it might be from the delinquent party. More than 60 percent of the customers said that they had overlooked payment and would send a check right away. And they did.

92. A store that had a lot of small invoices outstanding made up a miniature form that stated, "Since you only owe such a small amount, we thought that such a small reminder would be sufficient." Nearly all paid up.

93. Similarly, a credit manager sent out photocopies of an unmarked check made out to his company. The accompanying letter stated that this mystery check was received and he is wondering whether it belongs to the delinquent recipient. Out of 70 letters, 40 replies were received and 23 remittances.

94. A merchant who offered a 5 percent discount on cash purchases found that his cash sales increased from 54 percent to 72 percent.

95. One fashion store adds an alteration charge to the bill but removes it if the account is paid within 30 days.

96. A smart idea is to have a special section of merchandise prominently marked "Cash & Carry & Save."

97. A store that needed some part-time sales help during a busy season offered employment to delinquent customers—who then worked off their indebtedness.

98. In one small town, several merchants got together to "pool" delinquent accounts and then arranged with a bank to make consolidated loans to customers that merited it. This idea should be approached with caution.

99. Some stores send collection letters between Christmas and New Year's, suggesting that payment be made now as part of a New Year's resolution.

100. One merchant picks up considerable repeat business not only by sending out not only "paid" statements when a bill has been paid but also a special phone or mail-order offer. Customers, owing nothing to the store now, frequently order the offered item.

SALES AND FUND-RAISING | 8

TWENTY-FIVE PERSONAL POINTS ABOUT SELLING

Whatever your business, you will need to sell something. This goes for products, services—even selling yourself to a customer or client. Here is a set of common-sense "commandments" to help you make the most of your personal efforts.

1. *Smile.* It is the shortest route to a sale. The one overwhelming reason customers are turned off and there are no repeat sales is indifference on the part of the salesperson. A smile creates instant empathy. It says, "I like you."

2. *Be Helpful.* After the initial greeting, make your first question, "How can I help you?"

3. *Make Eye Contact.* Eyes are the window to our involvement as well as to our soul. Looking the prospect in the eyes shows your interest; looking away shows disinterest.

4. *Listen.* Find out what a customer has to say. Don't interrupt. Listening is more difficult than talking.

5. *Don't Argue.* You might not agree, but remember that the customer is always right.

6. *Be Accountable.* You are personally responsible for the sale and, therefore, for any of your actions that lead to the customer's satisfaction or dissatisfaction.

7. *Anticipate.* When the initial sale is completed, ask, "Is there anything else I can do for you?"

8. *Say Thanks.* Always thank the customer for his or her business. Even if you have to say *merci, danke, grazie, gracias, tak se meka, toda rabah, spaseebo, efcharisto, dank u, djekui.* It pays to learn these in our ethnic world.

9. *Ask for Suggestions.* Encourage customers, as well as employees and friends, to comment on your performance and your company's products.

10. *Use Them.* Don't just listen or observe, but make use of constructive suggestions and comments.

11. *Accept Complaints.* A "beef" is not completely negative; it is also an opportunity to improve.

12. *Resolve Problems.* Respond to complaints with a positive attitude, professionalism, and courtesy.

13. *Be Prompt.* Start the process of resolving the problem right away, before it festers into a sore.

14. *Show Willingness.* You can resolve the problem faster by listening politely and patiently than by resisting. This approach tends to take the wind out of the complainer's sails.

15. *Get All the Facts.* Ask specific and leading questions to show your concern and desire to solve the problem. You probably can't resolve every one you encounter, but you can try.

16. *Try to Understand.* Though you might not agree and might be frustrated, try to see the problem from the customer's perspective. One approach is to restate the problem the way the customer has phrased it.

17. *Set a Time Frame.* Get the complaining customer on your side by asking whether a specific time frame for resolution is okay.

18. *Follow Through.* See all problems through and make sure the buck is not passed.

19. *Apply Individualism.* Treat each complaint on its own merits; don't lump it with similar ones.

20. *Communicate.* When a resolution has been achieved, let the customer know about it as soon as possible.

21. *Check Back.* When the problem has been resolved, contact the customer by phone, in person, or with a response card to see that he or she is satisfied.

22. *Again, Say Thanks.* It won't hurt to let the customer know at the conclusion of this process that you appreciate his or her understanding and patience.

23. *Attend to Appearance.* The way your establishment looks, the way you look, the way your employees look set the tone for your company and products. This concept extends even to your delivery vehicle, stationery, and packaging.

24. *Other Nonverbals.* Besides appearance, there are traits and habits that can either impress or offend. A poor impression is made by smoking on the job, drinking, smelling badly, not getting up when the customer approaches, having unpleasant facial expressions, chewing gum or food, and slouching around instead of being attentive. The opposites of all these are ingredients that lead to sales and profits, satisfaction and happiness in business.

25. *Adopt This Customer Credo*:

Customers are the most important people we serve.

Customers are human beings with feelings like our own.

Customers deserve our courteous and attentive treatment.

Customers do not interrupt our work; they are the purpose of it.

Customers bring us their needs; it is our job to fulfill them.

Customers do not depend on us; we depend on them.

Customers are our business.

TEN WAYS TO BOOST SALES

The ideas below are particularly applicable to retail businesses. They are not entirely original, but they are a little different—and according to successful retailers, *they work*. For start-up businesses especially, these methods increase credibility and reportedly have increased sales two to two-and-a-half times over previous levels. Some of the approaches are equally applicable to service businesses.

1. *Cash Purchases*. If your business is based on billing, and there are expectations of 30 days' leeway, then getting cash on purchase or job completion is like getting 1 percent additional income—and probably more, since not everybody pays within 30 days. In fact, if you bill at the end of the month, and the customer takes a customary 30 days to pay, it could be as long as 60 days after the initial transaction before you will see any money. Let's say it costs you 12 percent to borrow money; then two months' worth of interest can be as much as 2 percent. Offer a 1 to 2 percent discount for cash payments and you will get a goodly portion of your business converted from charge to cash.

2. *Volume Purchases*. When customers buy in bulk you save money in service, handling, delivery, billing, and perhaps discounts

granted from your suppliers. Passing on all or some of these savings to the customer will encourage larger purchases and allow you to have greater merchandise turnover.

3. *Unadvertised Store Specials.* Numerous large chain and grocery stores make periodic in-store announcements on their public-address systems of special price reductions that were not advertised in other public media. If you do not have a PA system, you can top the discounted merchandising display with a bright card, stating "$AVE on this *Unadvertised* Special."

4. *Quick Delivery.* Quick or free delivery can make a difference in closing a sale. Some people are simply eager to receive their merchandise once they have purchased it; others must meet a deadline such as someone's birthday or anniversary. Often a charge can be made for this service, because the customer knows that "time is money."

5. *Advertising Enclosures.* These are piggyback mini-flyers that can be enclosed with statements and invoices. Since most billing mail weighs a mere half ounce, you can add another half ounce of promotional material without paying more postage. Remember, too, that your regular charge customer is probably the best repeat customer!

6. *Guaranteed Price.* This incentive is especially workable with industrial customers and buyers of commercial supplies. They might want to buy the items on February 15 but postpone delivery until after April 1, which is the time when they need the goods, or it is a new purchase/billing cycle or the time when they will open. Meanwhile, if they have locked in the price at current figures, you have created a happy customer.

7. *Rebate the Difference.* This assurance guarantees the buyer the lowest available price at this time. It states, in effect, that if the purchaser finds the identical item elsewhere at a lower price, and brings you proof within a certain time period, you will refund

the difference to your customer. Appliance dealers and jobbers use this method with telling success.

8. *Buy-Back.* This device is useful when selling pricey high-tech items that might be superseded by new models within a short time—computers or appliances are an example (although a sliding scale for usage might have to be applied). Jewelers who sell costly diamonds also use this device. In fact, some jewelers, confident that diamonds will only rise in value over the years, offer a full-price trade-in on a larger stone at any time in the future. The merchant loses nothing in the deal and usually can gain several years' appreciation on such a trade-in.

9. *Money-Back Guarantee.* This is the simplest and most common assurance of satisfaction: if the customer is not entirely happy with the purchase, he or she can bring it back either for full refund, proportionate refund (as with tires), or full credit on a replacement item. This device is almost mandatory on mail-order sales, but in reality few people take advantage of it.

10. *Double Your Money Back.* This approach effectively increases the previous "money-back guarantee" by 100 percent. But it also substantially increases sales, particularly of big-ticket items like major appliances or automobiles. While this idea might give some of your business associates conniptions, so few customers ever take advantage of it that its actual expense to the company in relation to its sales promotional value is insignificant.

NONPROFIT FUND-RAISING

It is not hardhearted to say that there is money to be made in nonprofit enterprises, too. From 10 to 90 percent of these organizations' collections—whether from contributions, items for sale, or games and contests in which prizes are awarded—goes toward overhead. The latter will include salaries to the operators, directors, or organizers. (Even charities, or promotional organizations that contribute a certain percentage to charities, have administrative people.) Some of these salaries are quite substantial, as you have learned from news reports about church-affiliated and masonic "nonprofit" organizations. Starting a nonprofit requires just as much time and effort as starting up a profit-oriented enterprise. It is a *business*, no matter how it is cloaked legally and via nomenclature. Unless you are rich enough to devote your time and talent on a volunteer basis to the promotion of your favorite church, charity, or social organization, the following list of fund-raising ideas can help you with a nonprofit, salary-paying enterprise of your own.

1. *Las Vegas Night*. This is one of the most profitable activities for fund-raising, although in some areas it is illegal, or permitted only with certain restrictions. There are many variations: usually an admission is charged, and food is sold for additional income. Payments are often handled in scrip or coupons. Wheels, games, and favors can be rented and purchased from novelty companies. As long as people go on loving to gamble, this will be one of the most popular ways of making a charitable donation.

2. *House Tour*. This activity is a favorite among women's organizations. Members who have opulent homes, especially those appointed by professional decorators, are solicited to play hosts. Other members are stationed in each room to guide traffic and act as guards. Maps are published with admission tickets. Free publicity is usually available in the women's and home sections of the local or neighborhood newspaper. Often an additional fund-raiser is held at night at the largest of the participating homes—a fancy cocktail party that is a $25 to $100 gala, and may showcase ladies' fashions as well. Prominent local decorators will cooperate, perhaps with a tour of their own homes. The annual Hadassah tour in Orlando, Florida—one of the most successful house tours—raises five-figure sums each year.

3. *Celebrity Golf Tournament.* The Baltimore, Maryland chapter of Save-A-Heart Foundation makes big bucks on this annual event, held at a local country club. Several famous golf and entertainment figures are invited to participate as guests and to make presentations to winners. The entry fee is quite steep and attracts the *crème de la crème* of local society and afficionados who want to be seen playing golf with the celebrities. Publicity is always heavy as are the net returns—which can go into six figures.

4. *Celebrity Ball.* Each year several hundred participants attend the Jewish National Fund (JNF) Blue-and-White-Ball in Baltimore, Maryland. A consistently good money raiser for the reforestation of Israel, this bash includes an all-out banquet, live orchestra, formal dress code, presence of leading political figures from the governor and a U.S. Representative on down, speeches and presentations, and always one or several honorees. With tickets costing in the $200 range, this event swells the JNF coffers by around $50,000 annually. Many charitable and nonprofit organizations (like friends of the local symphony and the Cancer Society) use this glamorous approach to annual buck-raising.

5. *Christmas Bazaar.* Among all holiday-themed fund-raisers, Christmas events probably lead in effective responses. The Symphony Bazaar held at Christmastime, in Birmingham, Alabama, for example, raises over $100,000 at what its sponsors claim is the biggest bazaar of its kind in the United States.

6. *Ethnic Festivals.* Invite various ethnic groups to show up in folk costumes, do their national dances, prepare and sell ethnic foods, and promote their activities. This, in turn, promotes yours, as well as attracting people to the neighborhood or municipality or shopping mall where the festival is held. Everyone involved benefits.

7. *Garden Show or Trip.* The annual Strawberry Festival in Orlando, Florida features lots of art exhibits, ethnic foods, and a lawn concert—all aimed at a yearly charity beneficiary that receives

the majority of the entrance fee. In another garden-oriented event, as a fund-raiser for a local public TV station, a travel agency promoted trips to the tulip fields and auction in Holland and to the Chelsea Garden Show in London. The station received $100 of the approximately $1500 cost of each trip, and the two tours attracted more than 140 participants.

8. *Art Auction*. This fund-raiser is popular in upper-middle-class suburbs, especially among synagogue memberships. The auctions usually are conducted by professional art dealers who travel to various locations, although local collectors or gallery owners also could handle them. It's fun for the participants and represents an easy 10 to 20 percent profit for the sponsoring synagogue, church, or organization. Each artwork offered has a "wholesale" starting point, of course, and the auctioneer better know his or her subject.

9. *Community White Elephant or Garage Sale*. This is especially good for closely knit communities, where participants can be reached easily and a good central location is available. Everybody has items in the attic, basement or closets that need to be eliminated in springtime, and this is a good way to both get rid of them and give to charity. Fresh Meadows, New York, for instance, has run a successful sale in which each neighbor "buys" standard printed tags to attach to the items to be sold at a central site. Neighborhood newspapers will publicize this kind of event widely. "Mystery packages" can add to the fun, as can an auctioneer, band, and refreshments for sale.

10. *Service Auction*. This event can work well in a middle- to upper-class organization. Members offer to perform a service for the winner of a "bid." Services include baby-sitting, housecleaning, hauling, letter writing, butlering, cooking, or—for commercial donors—catering, dry cleaning, etc. A Mount Vernon, New York, synagogue raised several thousand dollars at a single auction offering dozens of imaginative "services."

11. *Theater or Trip.* Tickets are sold to members for a special charitable performance, and the sponsoring organization gets a good percentage returned. Latching on to existing public concerts eliminates the risk of guaranteeing an audience minimum that might not be met.

12. *Cake Sales.* These are always popular but make for small fund-raisers (except for the Girl Scouts annual cookie sale). More money can be raised by putting a blank price sticker or sign on each cake or batch of cookies and then asking customers to pay whatever they think it is worth. Chances are they'll pay more than the normal price. *Cookbooks* are another popular way to raise money. Recipe contributors from an organization or congregation love "being published," and the sale of books at about double the production cost can go on for years. Publication can be celebrated at a charitable gourmet banquet, where some of the foods are served.

13. *Wine-and-food-tasting Party.* This kind of event is always popular and usually can be put on at no cost to the sponsors by a local vintner or shop. An Escondido, California, organization raised $25,000 with little investment, getting $15 per ticket.

14. *Nite at the Races.* This is similar to a Las Vegas Nite, but simpler to arrange. If you have a racetrack nearby, its clubhouse is an ideal location in which to stage this event. A rented film of a famed race can be shown. Entrants bet $2 at a window and get paid double their money if they are winners. A percentage from the concessionaire can add to the sponsor's kitty.

15. *Mock Arrests.* This requires the participation of prominent citizens who are held in a mock jail until their companies or families bail them out with a charitable donation, the amount of which is set ahead of time.

WOMEN ENTREPRENEURS

9

TWENTY-FIVE OF THE BEST BUSINESS OPPORTUNITIES

Gradual social changes or explosive technological changes can affect the businesses that women choose to enter. However, there are some career businesses that stand out among lesser lights. These are some of them:

1. *Business Doctors.* These are actual physicians who also have a sense of business operation. They might practice medicine, but they are mainly consultants to doctors with large practices, to Health Maintenance Organizations, and to hospitals. In addition to going through medical school and internship, the business doctor probably also has a Master's in Business Administration or Hospital Administration.

2. *HMO Executives.* They are consultants to the Health Maintenance Organizations that are springing up all over America.

Women who start such organizations or join a team that founds one can be in for a very rosy future. Health-care experience and marketing know-how are musts.

3. *Headhunters*. These professionals are more politely known as executive recruiters. They find top-notch personnel for industries where management is too busy to do it themselves or where the company prefers to keep a low profile. There are big fees in this business and start-up costs are low, though experience, connections, and credibility must be high.

4. *Executive Trainers*. These are consultants who seek a share in the $40-billion-a-year corporate-training industry. They are familiar with the latest sales techniques, effective management strategies, and newest computer software. Personal dynamism, established credibility, and good connections and education are required.

5. *Computer Consultants*. In the computer industry, this category has sprung up in the current generation. They advise on programs, act as liaisons between buyers and sellers, hold seminars. It is a very specialized and potentially remunerative business.

6. *Computer Lawyers*. This computer age that has been spawned also brings with it demand for new legal interpretations and methods of protection. Because of the very newness of this field, lawyers must sometimes be ahead of the law.

7. *Video Consultants*. These specialists are part trainers, part engineers, part public relations experts, part personnel experts. They produce video films for personnel recruiting, sales solicitations, stockholder presentations, and for whatever else is needed that video can do.

8. *Telecommunications Experts*. These people can be consultants or be part of a company producing and managing the vast array of communications media. Since the breakup of giant AT&T a few

years ago, a dizzying and seemingly never-ending array of opportunities has sprung up. Bell System experience is quite helpful.

9. *Information Center Operators*. Operating such centers for smaller firms and banks, or helping set up centers is another in the new genre of high-tech businesses. Computer knowledge is a must, as well as knowledge of information storage and sending. The best clients would be publishers, banks, and insurance and communications companies.

10. *Personnel Leasing*. This is a relatively new concept that goes a step beyond the "temp employment" agency. The idea started in the aerospace industry and others that are seasonal. The cost of training, hiring, and firing specialized personnel is prodigious; hence, many industries pay premium prices to "lease" personnel on an as-needed basis. The personnel firm pays all fees, salaries, and fringes—the client pays only the hourly or daily rate.

11. *Telemarketing*. Selling products by video has become a very large business, and it promises to increase substantially as more people work out of their homes or seek to avoid the crowds in downtown and mall shopping areas. This industry promises growth in catalog and direct-mail production.

12. *Financial Planners*. Currently, an estimated 300,000 such planners exist. Increased competition in the money management and lending field sparks the need for these experts. Companies often keep planners on retainer as advisers to their staffs, especially in the ever-changing tax areas.

13. *Mortgage Brokers*. In a sense, they are financial consultants, too. They find the right banks on the right terms and put them together with clients. The fee is about one-half of 1 percent of the amount of the mortgage. On $100,000, that will amount to $500—up front.

14. *Interest Rate Brokers*. This area is similar to the previous opportunity, except that these professionals bring corporations

and financial institutions together, and the figures go into the millions. They also deal with foreign investors, who are usually involved in trading short-term, variable deposits and long-term, fixed-rate assets. The industry is a mere five years old and earnings are high.

15. *Association Manager*. While this is generally a "hired" position, it ought to be mentioned. There are today about 20,000 trade, business, and professional associations, while a generation ago there were 5,000. You can form an association in any field not already covered or, if you have that background, act as adviser and consultant to those already in business.

16. *Sales Promotion Specialists*. In the last score of years, this corporate expenditure has risen 100 percent. Sales promotion agencies conduct contests, testimonial campaigns, new product introductions and promotions, and mail-order tests, and they analyze consumer buying trends. If you have an advertising and promotion background, this business could be satisfying and remunerative.

17. *Bank Marketing Specialists*. As an extension of the above business, the woman who has know-how and know-who in the banking profession can focus on this growing field. Bankers, especially independent ones, are beginning to think like merchandisers.

18. *Special Events Promoters*. There always have been women who put on fashion shows, shopping mall events, beauty contests, music festivals, and cultural events. But the emphasis on local image building is growing at the expense of paid media advertising. An SEP is a public relations person who specializes in staging events—much like a theatrical producer. The work can be profitable, hazardous, and fun.

19. *Image Consultants*. This is another public relations business with emphasis on creating a favorable image for a person or a

corporation, a politician or a town. Such identity specialists are psychologists, promoters, and writers, with just a little P.T. Barnum thrown in.

20. *Private School Operators.* Those in education with the credentials to start a small private school should look at the trends and figures. Today's day-care generation are tomorrow's private-school prospects. Many working parents are used to day-care costs, know some of the public-school shortcomings, and want a safe, academically high-quality, nondenominational school environment for their children.

21. *Athletic Consultants.* Athletically inclined? Despite the large number of two-breadwinner families, there are discernible trends both toward one parent staying at home and a decrease in health club memberships. Many people are buying at-home gym equipment. Check the trend.

22. *Retirement Planners.* Again, it's the statistics that dictate this category. Today's 30- to 40-year-old baby boomers are the next 50-year-old generation. Suddenly they will become conscious of those uncertain years ahead. College tuition costs, health-care needs, home-ownership equity, cruises and trips by themselves, cosmetic surgery, medical aging prevention, time-saving devices in the home, etc.—these are all factors the retirement financial planner takes into consideration.

23. *Specialty Merchandisers.* Whether in retailing or manufacturing, this is an age of specialization in products (though not necessarily in the services that go with them). With a broad and deep background in merchandising, a retailer or producer of a specialty product can gain quick attention in the marketplace, maintain a high profit margin, and blunt competitive pressures. Being something of an adventurer, a futurist, and a market researcher could also be helpful.

24. *Politicians.* There is no doubt about it, there is a growing number of women politicians on the local, state, and federal levels.

Women are perceptive, compassionate, people-oriented, and able to think beyond the individual to group needs. Women are learning to help one another, and that will be immeasurably beneficial to them in the political arena.

25. *International Business Operators.* Exporting and importing is not necessarily a "women's business," but it is a woman's opportunity. Besides being a national goal, exporting is a challenging, interesting, and complicated business as our world becomes more global.

NEW BUSINESSES AND TIPS ON EXPORTING

10

NINETEEN BUSINESS IDEAS FROM JAPAN

While Americans are not short on inventiveness, the Japanese have been ultrabusy coming up with ingenious ways to separate surplus yen from their citizens. Here are a few of them that might be worth a second thought—or serious investigation.

1. *Maze Amusement Park.* It covers an area of a football field and can take from 12 minutes (the record time) to five hours to traverse. There are emergency exits for those who develop claustrophobia, control stations manned by attendants, theme displays, and even prizes for those who get through the maze in excellent times. The maze is so popular in Osaka and Kyoto that clubs have been formed, and school children take group outings to them.

2. *Sneak-y Washers.* Athletic footwear is very popular in Japan, too. However, sneakers do get dirty and sometimes smelly. Now special automatic washer-dryers have been developed that clean

athletic shoes. It is an innovation that might go over well in the many athletic footwear stores here.

3. *Hello, Beautiful.* Some telephone booths in the Land of the Rising Sun are equipped with mirrors. The caller can primp for a date while making arrangements on the phone. This would also provide an opportunity to place small ads around the mirror.

4. *Toilet-Sink.* A compact toilet bowl has been designed whose tank has a spigot on top. Water for washing hands runs into the tank and is used for flushing. Thus, space is saved, as well as water, and installation is simplified. It can be ordered from Toto-Kiki, Inc., Tokyo, in two-gallon and four-gallon sizes.

5. *Luxury Cabs.* While many American taxis are the pinnacle of discomfort, Japanese taxis are loaded with comforts. Imagine how a taxi company in the United States would fare if its vehicles featured, as many Japanese cabs do: clean, linen-covered headrests; doors that swing open and shut automatically; automatic tapes that say "thank you" and ask "have you forgotten anything in the cab?"; pay TV in the passenger compartment; vibrator seats that soothe tired bodies—and even polite drivers who wear white gloves.

6. *A Moving Experience.* If you ever have moved, chances are that you have some gripes about broken items, lost boxes, dirt tracked in, or time delays. In Osaka, Japan, there is a moving company run by a woman who moves people with empathy. The huge van contains a fully equipped, miniature studio room above the driver's cab, where the family can rest, watch TV, and get drinks—traveling comfortably in the same van as their completely boxed and fumigated belongings. For moving into a second-story home, there's even a van that lifts up to that level and delivers through the windows.

7. *Drink n' Drive Service.* Cops in Japan are a lot tougher on inebriated drivers than in the United States. Hence, a service has

developed, costing only 20 to 25 percent above the cost of a taxi ride, that dispatches two escorts to the scene of a celebration. While one escort takes the happy drunk home, the other follows in the customer's car, leaving it in front of his or her domicile. The service is handled mainly by bartenders and caterers. Can't you just imagine "Seagram's Sotted Service" becoming a 100-proof hit in America?

8. *A People Bank.* Imagine yourself going into a bank on any Friday to deposit your paycheck. A polite clerk records your deposit as you enter, and you then sit down in the lounge to have a cup of tea or watch TV. In a little while, your name is called out and your receipt or deposit book returned to you. All your home and utility bills can be paid by the bank, and there are teller machines that accept both bills and coins and enter the amount into your deposit book. If an American bank were to render such service, which is available in Tokyo, they could probably reduce interest one-half percent and still have depositors crowding in.

9. *At Your Service, Ah So.* As they, like we, are becoming more and more of a service-based economy, the Japanese *benriya-san* business is booming. This is an agency (in Tokyo there are at least 500 of them) that really does everything for you: walks your dog, pays your bills, does your shopping, stands in for you at funerals, even writes and delivers speeches, plays ball with your kids, and takes care of minor repairs around the house. The charge, at current rates, is about $12 to $24 per hour. Of course, you've got to have a yen for such charges.

10. *Beauty, Beauty on the Wall.* Are you going to be the best tressed of them all? Some big-city beauty parlors in Japan have computerized TV monitors that can show your face framed with any one of 300 different hair styles. That way, you can pick a style before the operator starts cutting—and know how you will look later. The beautician then works by the numbers. The cost of the magic machine is about $400 a month from a company named E.R.C., Inc.

11. *Ideas for Eateries*. Restaurants are the most frequently opened new businesses in America, and perhaps in the world—and also the most frequently closed. To see some unusual eateries, take a look around Tokyo, where you will find the following: clusters of mini bars, often dozens together, usually run by a female hostess; luxury bars where regular customers have their own bottles, marked with their names; restaurants where the arriving guest is offered a hot, moist napkin to wipe face and hands, and where realistic plastic models of various dishes on the menu are displayed; home or office delivery of hot foods in real glass dishes; intimate little restaurants for lovers; eateries with couches for very tired workers or night owls who want a half-hour rest; *kissaten* (coffee shops, of which Tokyo alone has about 30,000) that feature different kinds of music (you can make requests, too); a bar that has a creek running through it, carrying dozens of appetizing hors d'oeuvres on platters—you just grab one and pay $2. So where's our Yankee ingenuity?

12. *Telephone Secretary*. If you don't have a personal secretary, you can pick up the phone in Tokyo and call your secretarial service. On the phone you dictate your previous day's activities, meeting memos, or anything else of which you need a record. In a relatively short time a transcript is on your desk.

13. *Wanna Buy a Duck?* What with so many American family farms in trouble, here's an idea from crowded Japan: Farmers sell a live turkey or growing apple tree to some city slicker, but the bird and the tree stay on the farm. When Thanksgiving time comes, that turkey is slaughtered and sent, fresh from the farm, to the city "stockholder." Ditto for apples and a whole lot more.

14. *Hi-fidelity Salesmanship*. We Americans pride ourselves on our ability to sell. Yet, if you are planning to go into the sales representation business, or, specifically, sell VCRs, Camcorders, and similar high-tech equipment, you might take a look at what aggressive Japanese companies are doing. Take the example of a

camera company in Osaka. One of its sales promotion methods is to maintain a booth at a local theme park, where it rents video cameras. A salesperson shows the tape to the proud father after the tour, and 30 to 60 days later, a call back and home demonstration usually result in a sale.

15. *Mobotron: Have Motor, Will Travel.* A Japanese invention, Mobotron is a giant 10 × 13 ft. screen that is mounted on the side of a truck. The screen displays a film or commercial. The vehicle travels along a specific route of the client's choice, or it can be stationed in one place at important events or be mobile. The cost in high-priced Tokyo is $8000 a day, including truck and driver.

16. *Stop-a-Crime.* In Tokyo, an ingenious supplier of items for the police department came up with a metal, life-size reproduction of a policeman. He sold them to the police department and to banks, which put these two-dimensional cops at key locations. While everybody knows they are only metal replicas, they seem to have a psychological impact that has resulted in fewer automobile accidents and robberies. Know anyone in *your* police department who might be interested?

17. *Mini Photo Lab Miracle.* Developed by Noritsu America, the fully automated photo-developing machine has been a tremendous success since 1978 when the first Ritz store opened with it. Everything is computerized, and quality is generally high. While a big stumbling block may be the $100,000-plus initial investment, terms can be arranged. Breakeven is reached quickly—according to some owners, in only three months. Profitable locations are in mall shopping centers, where customers can leave their rolls of film, shop for an hour, then come back for the finished product—at a cost of about $10.

18. *Out-of-Town Hospitality Service.* For about $10,000 cash you can set up a service that takes care of tourists and convention visitors. It involves having a passenger van, an office location, and a promotion plan. You make arrangements with hotels and

convention centers; provide a driver (unless YOU are the driver) who knows your town well; and plan an itinerary of sightseeing, lectures-as-you-go, good places to have reasonable lunches, great stores to shop—and you'll have happy customers. Some "tips" might be involved to bell captains and convention managers, but then this will cut down on advertising costs.

19. *Catering to the Handicapped.* A man in Osaka, Japan, opened a store that caters solely to handicapped citizens, carrying ponchos that can cover those in wheelchairs, single shoes, ramps to fit over stairs, and more, and he offers custom tailoring adjustments. Customers are referred by doctors, hospitals, manufacturers of special railings and other orthopedic necessities, etc. The company is on its way to becoming a national business through publicity and mail order.

TWELVE TIPS FOR GOING INTO EXPORTING*

With U.S. government pronouncements about America's imbalance of trade being almost daily fodder for the news columns, it is no wonder that Uncle Sam in encouraging small manufacturers, wholesalers, and distributors to look into export as a way of expanding their own fortunes—and of correcting our lopsided, national trade balance. Virtually every department in the government—federal and state—offers some help in getting the small export entrepreneur started. The assistance you can get from specific country information directors at the U.S. Department of Commerce via brochures is prodigious. Here are just a few points to consider before you leap into overseas marketing.

1. *Qualified Export Counseling.* Get yourself an export manager who can guide you in developing a master strategy and international marketing plan.

* See also numerous "Success Stories" in Part Two, for dramatic examples of export achievements.

2. *Full Management Decision.* There is no sense in starting to export your products or services without the full support and commitment of all of your people, and that includes a financial commitment. It's a whole new business and demands the same effort you probably applied to your business in the first place.

3. *Overseas Reps.* Getting the right people to represent you overseas is vital. You won't be there most of the time. Rely on commercial reps in the United States and your local counselor to guide you properly and help you execute the right agreements.

4. *Concentration of Operation.* The initial temptation is to grab export offers from anywhere in the world; however, that dilutes your effectiveness and could spread your resources too thin. It's difficult enough to learn about the idiosyncracies of one nation or region. Establish a basis for profitable operation in one country or region at a time.

5. *Domestic Interference.* If you have been used to working with domestic sales, you might tend to favor these the minute export selling becomes tough or troublesome. Don't do it. Most corporations have discovered that overseas sales are more profitable and collection problems invariably are nil.

6. *Fair Treatment for Overseas Contacts.* If a problem situation crops up, your instincts might be to give your overseas reps and customers second-rate treatment. This is another pitfall to avoid, for it will spell disaster. You need to treat these people on an equal basis with their domestic counterparts at all times.

7. *Marketing Differences.* Don't assume that selling techniques will be alike on both sides of the ocean. Social and economic conditions, likes and dislikes, are as different from those in the United States as speech and food. Your marketing techniques must be tailored to each country—which is why a knowledgeable export counselor is so necessary. To proceed otherwise could be embarrassing and disastrous.

8. *Product Flexibility.* Overseas regulations might be different from those in the domestic market. Listen to your advisors and make your own observations regarding regulations and cultural preferences in other countries. Sizes, measurements, colors, packaging, imprinting, instructions, and pricing are just some of the factors to be analyzed, as well as the terms of sales and promotion.

9. *Clear Warranties.* Because you are marketing a product or service overseas, giving an assurance of product quality is doubly important. You are operating at arm's length, so to speak, and your warranty must be clearly stated and must be printed in the language of the country in which you are selling.

10. *Export Management.* Because the marketing problems overseas are so different and because these differences are often quite subtle, hiring an experienced export-management company should definitely be considered—especially if you are not big enough to afford your own on-premise expert, or if you have been unsuccessful in previous export attempts.

11. *Joint Venturing.* When dealing overseas, the law might require you to enter into an agreement with an indigenous business entity. You can do this by joint venture, by licensing, or by having a foreign trading corporation set up by you.

12. *Servicing.* If servicing your products is important in this country, it is even more important when selling overseas. Parts must be available and trained service personnel in place if you are going to inspire confidence in your products, keep them functioning, and assure repeat sales. It is common in many less developed countries for local operators to be technically undertrained, to give up too easily, and to be underfinanced and unable to afford replacement parts and servicing. The evidence is the inoperative machinery cluttering the roadsides, alleys, and backyards in these countries. If you want to have more than a one-shot business, then servicing must be built into the marketing effort.

Part Two

Success Stories

INTRODUCTION: TAPPING INTO THE FUTURE

The years left before this millennium turns into the twenty-first century are seeing a few changes in existing enterprises and the addition of new ones. Capitalism is beginning to display a more benevolent face, so that many of these businesses are, or at least start out to be, geared toward a more socially conscious world and to the preservation of our environment and ecology. Others are just ideas whose time has come.

What follows, first, are some suggestions for future businesses, based on perceived social trends generally and trends toward ecologically and socially oriented enterprises. The next group of 60-plus brief narratives are actual case histories of successes that have been achieved to date by imaginative and hard-working entrepreneurs.

TEN BUSINESSES FOR THE NEXT DECADE

The Baby Boom Business

Somehow, despite the growing incidence of professional couples, childless couples, and alternative couples, the number of babies born keeps increasing. Biology has a way of defying dire predictions, and that augurs well for businesses that cater to babies and their parents. The Juvenile Products Manufacturers Association reports that the future looks pink (and blue) indeed. The annual business done by its members is nearly $2 billion.

A Future in Back-to-Crafts

As our world becomes more and more sophisticated and robotized, a reverse trend is simultaneously noticeable. Arts and crafts shows are attracting huge crowds. While some people are constantly looking for high-tech innovations to make their modern, hectic lives easier, others are reverting to the ways their elders used to make things—laboriously, ingeniously, by hand. They practice or appreciate "folk arts" and buy hand-made goods.

Customizing the Car

Shops that put special custom touches on ordinary cars have been around for quite a few years. But the evidence is that this trend is growing by leaps and bounds. There are several distinct markets, and thus opportunities, for the handy-Andy mechanic: (1) custom conversions of standard models into convertibles—this is being done by such giants as Ford who contract out to smaller auto-body shops to handle the conversions individually, because it is more economical; (2) custom alterations such as installing a sun roof, a special grille, an external spare-tire well, supercharger tubes, or extra springs; (3) car assembly kits that provide the buyer with a 1929 Bugatti body and a VW chassis, for instance, giving owners a look of distinction for $15,000 instead of the collector's price of $45,000. This business is a by-product of our age of opulence.

Dollars in the Dumps

Every state in the country has the same problems: a growing mountain of garbage, coupled with inadequate facilities for disposal. An entrepreneur who can come up with practical ways of improving garbage disposal, with more biodegradable products, with secondary re-use of waste products (such as recycling of paper and plastic products) can cash in prodigiously. Many states now make money available for research on this problem. At the head of these efforts is Florida. In any one year, around 35,000,000 tourists flock into Florida—and many thousands stay permanently. This means millions more tons of paper and plastic refuse and fewer and fewer places to bury the stuff in this flat state. The State Legislature is looking at entrepreneurial incentives to turn waste into useful products. There might not be any gold in them thar Florida hills, but there could be lumps of loot in their dumps.

Ecology Businesses

A new generation of marketers is developing. They try to incorporate into their products and services a social consciousness and a deep concern for our environment. They look for products that can be powered by solar cells (watches, calculators, personal appliances, etc.); materials that can be recycled or are biodegradable; devices that eliminate toxicity from water, air, and homes; devices that conserve water and energy.

Two organizations that are working in this area and that welcome participation include the Council on Economic Priorities, 30

Irving Place, New York, NY 10003; and Niche Marketing Services, 126 Intervale Rd., Burlington, VT 05401. Both publish newsletters or catalogues.

This new-age consciousness also has spawned several investment groups and mutual funds that specialize in "socially responsible" capitalism. A $5.00 booklet called "Socially Responsible Financing Planning Guide" is available from Co-Op America, 2100 M St., NW, Suite 310, Washington, DC 20063.

Fast Food of the Future

Considering the recent proliferation of fast-food restaurants, you might think we have reached a saturation point. No way. According to a National Restaurant Association report, the trend toward eating out or buying prepared foods will continue. However, there are some caveats that you should observe and incorporate into any plans you might have for opening or expanding a restaurant. Because of the importance of service and pitfalls involved in having servers, many restaurants are switching to buffet-style self-service that requires fewer hard-to-get good personnel. Plastic utensils and packaging will probably have to be biodegradable in the future, because our nation can no longer accommodate all the garbage and trash that are being generated. Shortages of potable water, and the deterioration of some water supplies, already make it necessary for some restaurants to install water-purification equipment or limit the serving of water unless asked for.

The Latest Scoop

You wouldn't expect ice cream purveyors to have a brilliant future—what with cholesterol and obesity warnings in the news daily. But the facts speak for themselves: small increases in ice-cream consumption are recorded each year. More than $9 billion worth of the delicious frozen dessert is consumed in the United States annually. The premium (that is, richest) ice creams are now getting 38.5 percent of the total market. Despite the plethora of gourmet flavors, vanilla is still the all-time favorite by a four-to-one margin over the next preference, chocolate. Lots of franchises are available at varying rates. At the same time, to answer health concerns, many new frozen desserts are coming on the market and are likely to grow in popularity—including lower-cholesterol products like frozen yogurt, and nondairy products like Tofutti. And if business gets a little slow, you can always eat the inventory.

No Place Like Home

Home delivery of prepared meals and/or groceries is also a comet among food businesses. The call for this service has been zooming upward in most cities because (1) more elderly people are living alone and do not want to or cannot cook for themselves any longer; (2) more family units consist of working couples, and having a prepared meal delivered is almost a necessity; (3) casual and ethnic foods are gaining in popularity everywhere, led by pizza pies and Chinese carry-out; (4) well-heeled professional couples see it as a mark of success and luxury to which they are entitled, to pick up the phone and order a couple of bags of gourmet groceries, or meals, or anything else their hearts and stomachs desire. In 1990, the market for home-delivered food is expected to top $10 billion, growing a sensational 30 percent annually. In the next few years, predictors say, as much as 25 percent of the eat-out market will be a home-delivered, eat-in market. So if you're looking for a new business to get into, remember what the good witch said to Dorothy in *The Wizard of Oz*: "There's no place like home."

Religious Retailing

Part of the new wave is a tremendous revival in religious merchandise in the United States. Like any retail operation, this one requires careful planning and adequate financing—at least $50,000. But the profits can be high. There are fewer markdowns and sales needed and less likelihood of obsolescence than in other retailing. You need to know your merchandise, whatever the denomination. Some franchises exist already in this field, and numerous wholesalers and specialty magazines attest to the tremendous potential of the religion-oriented market. Big items, popular in all faiths, are books and jewelry. The inspirational industry today is a $20-billion-plus business.

Testing the Tanks

Food and fuel are the two major necessities. Several suggestions have been devoted to the former. Regarding the latter, a business that will be growing mightily in the next decade is gasoline-tank testing, repairing, and replacement. There are more than 700,000 gasoline storage facilities in the United States, containing over two million buried gas tanks. As these age, some of the tanks begin to leak and infuse gasoline into the groundwaters that are then pumped into kitchen water systems. It is very costly to filter this water, besides being risky. So now state legislatures and the EPA are getting tough about this problem. In California and New York laws have already been enacted and stiff fines levied for faulty installations. The demand to test and, where necessary, to repair or replace these tanks will increase. Forget about tigers; there are plenty of bucks in those tanks for the alert entrepreneur.

BRIEF CASE HISTORIES OF
SMALL BUSINESS SUCCESSES

ADVERTISING AGENCY: GROWTH BY BOARD

A moderate-sized advertising agency operated by two young women in St. Paul, Minnesota, had reached an impasse. It happens to many small businesses: an apparent brick wall rises up to block further progress—combined with limited capital, overwhelming "housekeeping" problems and lack of outside input. Having heard about a consulting organization named SCORE, one of the young partners approached the local chapter with an idea. What about getting a team of their experts together as an advisory board of directors to see whether they could resolve some of the inevitable growth problems that beset small businesses at a certain stage of their development? And this is exactly what happened. The local SCORE office fielded a team of volunteers with a range of expertise. They suggested that a business plan be drawn up that showed unequivocally where the ad agency wanted to go. They set up a system of analysis to chart profitable growth, a marketing plan to develop new business, and a management plan that allowed for new creative help to be acquired as new income warranted it. The planning paid off. Within a three-year period, the agency's billing increased from $4.2 million to $13.2 million.

AEROBICS FOR PROFIT

Look at what Jacki Sorenson started! Her baby, aerobics, has been popular for a number of years now, and no wonder—more than half of the American population is overweight. To aid the trend, doctors and nutritionists have declared aerobics to be good exercise. Perhaps not for all, but for those who enjoy activity, it's a great business both in terms of fitness and finances. If you're into doing aerobics and have a couple of thousand dollars, this might be the business to consider: a rented hall, a tape recorder/player with the right kind of bouncy music, some signs around the supermarket, a few calls on women's clubs in your area, some studying of literature on the subject—and voila! Better be sure to have liability insurance coverage. Bring-a-friend promotions are good, as aerobics is sort of a friendly activity. You might consider, as several successful operators have done, adding nutrition counseling and baby-sitting service while moms are hopping for health. Think also in terms of coeducational clients. You might canvass your initial audience to see how they feel about that. What will attract more of them—privacy or sex appeal? One, two, cha cha cha . . . .

AGRICULTURE: E PLURIBUS UNUM FARMING

In the past couple of decades, small farms have been falling like straws in the wind. Mergers, flights to the city, and competition have taken their toll. Yet, there is a discernible trend, a revival, of the minifarm, and any agriculturally inclined entrepreneur or ag-college graduate ought to explore this phenomenon. In the Virginia–Maryland area, a number of minifarms have sprung up, survived, and even become successful. They are hydroponic and organic vegetable operations that can be as tiny as one-third of an acre or as "gigantic" as six acres.

What makes them profitable for their owners is an improved distribution system. Organic Farms of Beltsville, Maryland, distributes organically grown produce from the Carolinas to Maine. The company not only buys from many smaller growers in its market, it runs seminars to help them manage more efficiently; provides experts to teach them quality control; and provides uniform boxes, hard-to-find organic fertilizers, and the kind of respect that makes for a partner relationship rather than a dog-eat-dog competition. Waterfield Farms in Chantilly, Virginia, provides similar support to its hydroponic produce suppliers. With the backing and muscle of its big parent company, Weyerhauser, Waterfield has ways and means to improve its suppliers' production, assure year-round distribution, and even provide financing when this becomes necessary. Bob Cheves, one of its small suppliers in Delray, West Virginia, summed it up like this: "It's an ideal arrangement for me . . . small growers must have a way to market cooperatively." Amen.

ARCHITECTURAL SERVICE: BUILDING SUCCESS

In 1978, Penny Kerry's boss died. She had been secretary and right hand to a San Francisco architect and not having an architectural degree did not stop the determined woman from trying to carry on the firm. Legal tangles developed that caused her to withdraw—but not in defeat. With two other former employees she started PNI Omnitechts, a company that provides all the architectural functions of the previous firm but goes a few steps further. PNI designs, builds, and furnishes the jobs it obtains.

Thus there is only one source of responsibility, and clients like that. Since occasional loans are needed to maintain long-term projects, convincing bank loan officers has been the firm's biggest challenge. "They still assume that if you're a woman, you ought to run a boutique," Kerry observes. Banks are usually attuned to hard assets, and service companies don't have that, so they are more difficult to assess. Still, persistence and a steady growth record based on servicing clients to the hilt has boosted the woman-led company into the $5 million range, and a brand new project obtained last year could change that to the $10 million range. $10 million in 10 years is a pretty good building record!

AUTOMOTIVE: THREE STORIES

Auto Detailing

This is a low-start-up, high-net-profit business that can be started in any high-traffic location, and it is growing by leaps and bounds. One ambitious entrepreneur has brought his automobile beauty shop to area new-car dealers as well as used-car operators. Another has acquired a mobile unit that goes directly to the client to wax, polish, and detail his or her car while the customer works or is at home watching television. Gimmicks such as placing flyers under windshields at parking lots and garages offering to "make your car whistle-clean while you work" (cutting in the attendant for a quick "fiver") got lots of business. Another operator printed up guaranteed-satisfaction certificates that allowed a discount on subsequent detailing services. Still another tied in with a well-located quick-lube station. As cars escalate into the $15,000 to $20,000 price bracket, owners won't mind investing $100 to $200 periodically to keep their rolling stock at peak value, at least cosmetically.

From Rubles to Riches

This is a typical Horatio Alger story of the 20th century: Artur Lukowski, a Russian immigrant who came to our shores with $20 in his pocket, struggled for years until the light finally came on with a flash. A new business idea was implemented, and 30-some years later, he is a millionaire. The business, Oil Express, is one that is now quite familiar to us—a quick-lubrication service. The special point about this Gary, Indiana-based operation is that its owner started small, did lots and lots of research and traffic studies before he leased his first location, worked hard, saved his bucks, and expanded step by step with nary a loan.

His first location has serviced well over 300,000 cars, and it has been joined by more than three dozen others. The owner's 30-year-old son is now in the business as operations manager and shares his dad's penchant for total honesty with the customers. You always get what you ask for and expect—and that includes a choice of 37 brands of oil, and filters available for every car on the road. There's always a good cup of coffee awaiting the customer, too. Perhaps most impressive of all is a highly polished training system that turns green young employees into efficient public relations representatives. The concrete result of this philosophy is more than 650,000 gallons of Quaker State motor oil used each year. And at the bank—well, the few rubles the young émigré started with have turned into many U.S. dollars.

From Despair to Truck Repair

A funny thing happened to Greg Wagner of Dubuque, Iowa, on his way to the local unemployment office. A truck repairman, he had been laid off by the John Deere Company, and here he was, a mature man going to collect a state dole. Before he got there, however, he ran into a friend who also repairs trucks. This friend was in business for himself and told Greg how some counselors for the SCORE office had encouraged him to try it. So instead of going to unemployment, Wagner stopped off at the SCORE office. Luckily, the man on duty that day was a retiree from John Deere, and with the latter's advice and encouragement, a lot of additional guidance, and hard work, the ex-Deere truck repairman became an entrepreneur. Now he repairs semis from Chicago to Des Moines, and his reputation for quality work is spreading. He even has been able to acquire a mobile service truck at a cost of $40,000 and has hired his third employee. Looking beyond, Wagner is studying the advantages of franchising as one way to expand his business and his income.

BAKERY: FOUR STORIES

Sweet Tooth Is Recession Proof

John Barricelli, 29, a professional baker, owns his own shop in Brooklyn, New York. A couple of years ago, when he wanted to fly on his own, he learned that to open the kind of first-class bakery he felt customers in his area would expect could take $100,000. Luckily, he had a cousin who had the "dough." In the first year of business, Cousin John's Cafe & Bakery grossed $360,000. But to achieve this, John put in so many 18-hour days that his partner–cousin bought him a cot for Christmas so he could sleep in the back of the store.

For the record, Cousin John has been immensely successful for at least three good reasons: (1) he loves what he is doing and is good at it; (2) he worked very hard to get the business off the ground; (3) he produced a superior selection of pastries that brought customers back again and again, regardless of the vagaries of the economy.

Fruit Cakes Selling Like Hot Cakes

Until Famous Amos came along with his chocolate-chip cookies, it was usually women one heard about turning a baking sideline into a successful commercial business. In Adelphi, Maryland, Art Whitaker recently changed a Christmastime fruitcake-baking hobby into a genuine enterprise. His light and delicious cakes had been famous for 20 years, but only among a select number of friends, when he finally was persuaded to spread the goodness more widely. Friends took the idea to the Graduate School of Business at American University in Washington, DC, where students thought this was a very sweet idea.

Someone approached the prestigious department store, Bloomingdale's, which agreed to test-market the Whitaker cakes. The first batch sold out quickly, and, before you could say yum-yum, a hundred more were ordered. With the help of Bloomingdale's, Whitaker designed an elegant package and held a contest to rename the confection. They picked the appealing name "Rumfru Delight" because the cakes contained both rum and fruit. Even at the $20 to $25 price, Whitaker's light fruit cakes are expected to be heavy sellers next year. "My projection for next year is to produce 5000 cakes," says Art Whitaker, 46-year-old entrepreneur, who might well have to turn his weekend avocation into a full-time vocation. Now he can have his cake and eat well, too!

The Cake Is in the Mail

Another invention-by-necessity business has developed in Boulder, Colorado. Debora Tsakoumakis was trying to send a birthday cake to her father in Los Angeles. After a frustrating round of phone calls in which she tried to find a bakery in that city that would deliver a cake to her dad, she knew that a new business was crying to be born. She got an 800 number, a VISA credit-card account, and formed HB Bakery Connection. In her local library she researched the names and addresses of bakeries across the country. Soon she had nearly 150 bakeries in more than 40 states signed up. She charges the bakery no fee for the service but asks each participant to display a poster in the store declaring itself a member of this telephone network—just as florists have been doing for many years. Each delivered cake is personalized and delivered fresh from the local bakery. The cost to the client is $35 per cake, which gives the participating bakery full retail price plus delivery reimbursement—and provides a profit for HB Bakery Connection. Start-up costs were minimal—under $2000, and the outcome was a business that can be operated from home with very sweet results.

Fills Hole in Bagel Business

Allen Kent and several partners had an idea that the demand for bagels could be enlarged if they could furnish partially baked bagels to retailers across the nation. Of course, bagel giants such as Lender's and Sara Lee were in the business on a grand scale. However, venture capitalists who were approached by the Kent group agreed that the $620-million bagel market was worth biting into. The partners started the Big Apple Baking Company in Brooklyn, New York in 1985. Their "New Yorker" bagel is a four-inch partially baked beauty that is blast frozen and then shipped off to supermarket bakeries throughout the country.

Within three years, Big Apple reported $2.5 million in sales coming out of their 16,000-square-foot facility, which is operated by 45 employees. In the case of Big Apple, a David took on the Goliaths of the industry, and by dint of being just a little bit better and harder working, achieved success in a relatively brief period of time. They are having to share some of the gains with venture capitalists, of course. But that's the way the bagel rolls.

A BANK THAT THINKS SMALL

In these days of megamergers, it is unique to find a banking business that has decided "small is better." The National Security Bank in Toledo, Oregon, an independent financial institution, decided to issue its own VISA and Mastercards rather than tying in with a gigantic, out-of-area banking system. It is offering the credit cards for $15 a year, at an annual interest rate of 15 percent. Some good, local banking customers who had been turned down by national credit-card operators were very pleased. One hundred and seventy private and 20 commercial customers signed up in quick order. NSB simplified the language of its agreements, too, and began an energetic program of soliciting depositors and borrowers. The bank's Don Hoshino expects the first 500 accounts to be the break-even point. This kind of decentralization proves that the minnow still has a chance, even in the same sea with a whale.

A BEAUTY SHOP BONANZA

Small entrepreneurs who want to open a beauty salon, or be successful in one, need to know about business methods. The year that Delores Lowell opened Parklawn Hair Salon in Minneapolis, Minnesota, she was able to bring in only $4000 profit. Such "progress" would quickly put her out of business, because she, like other start-up entrepreneurs, had overlooked one of the largest single expense items in a business: the living salary of the owner. Clearly, $4000 was not enough for eating and paying the rent, too. A call to the local Service Corps of Retired Executives office was answered by two women volunteers who provided free help, especially in financial management. The counselors provided managerial and financial advice, as well as motivation to continue on. Ms. Lowell stayed in business and prospered. Within a few short years she employed seven operators and was grossing nearly

$150,000. Beauty shop operators, like artists, are not always the best business people, for creative minds do not always tend in a practical direction. But as the Minneapolis Ms. discovered, proper business organization is as necessary as satisfied clients.

BOOKS: A LIBRARY FOR $69.50

Just a few years ago, Cynthia J. Folino had a good idea. She noted an increase in book sales at the same time that people were getting busier and busier and complaining of their lack of time. She decided to produce summaries of books that would be important for busy executives to know about. She founded Executive Book Summaries in 1978, which sends digests of many business books each month to thousands of executive readers. For an annual subscription rate of $69.50, EBS brings a veritable business library into the offices and homes of those who want to be kept abreast of new business developments but don't have time to plow through the hundreds of books put out each year by dozens of publishers. After ten years of working at promoting this idea, she is now grossing more than $1.5 million annually. As Ms. Folino says, "It was a good idea implemented by good people." EBS is located at 5 Main Street, Bristol, VT 05443.

CANVAS COMPANY COVERS THE MARKET

Out in southern North Dakota and northern Minnesota, the winters can get pretty rough. Farm machinery that is not protected suffers. That's how Ed Shorma figured it when he decided to go into the business of manufacturing canvas tarps in his area. In 1956, he started on a very small scale making canvas protective covers for farm trucks, grain drill boxes, and fertilizer attachments. Fourteen years later, he was ready to go full tilt into expanding his business. By showing that he could produce extra sales and employment providing canvas seats for Canadian farm-equipment makers, he was able to swing a $75,000 loan through SBA channels. At that time, the little outfit, then called Wahpeton Canvas Company, was employing 17 local folks and doing a mere $147,000 in business annually. With the SBA-backed seed money, he was able to grow to the point where the Shorma Company (as it is now called), employs 220 people and grosses more than $12 million a year. It seems that the SBA has indeed un-cover-ed a goldmine in North Dakota.

CHARCOAL: MAKE IT MESQUITE

During the last decade or so, mesquite charcoal has surfaced as something of a deluxe cooking medium in steak houses. But one time it was almost frowned upon. A company in the San Francisco Bay area had a tough time with it until a business consultant made some merchandising suggestions. He noted that the charcoal burns at 1700 degrees F instead of at the 700 degrees of ordinary charcoal. This would sear the meat or fish quickly and seal in the natural juices as well as the flavors. He had the company repackage the product and present it as a cooking ingredient instead of as a fuel. Under this approach, mesquite charcoal became the "in" product of the barbecue industry, and sales took off. Sometimes taking an ordinary item and "discovering" a unique property will not only glamorize the product but energize lagging sales.

CONSTRUCTION: TWO STORIES

Minority Builder Is Major Success

When *Hispanic Business* magazine named Maya Construction/Ruiz Engineering "the fastest-growing Hispanic-owned company in Arizona" (November 1986), it touched on a business success story of enormous proportions. Roberto Ruiz grew up in Nogales, in the Sonora province of Mexico. He was able to emigrate to Tucson, Arizona, attend the University of Arizona there, and be graduated as a civil engineer. After working first for the state and then for a private firm, he went into business for himself in 1977, hiring two employees. A dozen years later, he employs over 250 people and has expanded so much that he can no longer be classified as a "small business."

However, back in 1978, when Ruiz was able to get minority certification under the 8(a) Program, his sales were $1,748. Within the first decade as an independent company, he received well over $60 million worth of government contracts. He built schools, water systems, private and public buildings, and roadways and sewers, and he worked his way to an annual volume of around $25 million. Initially, the SBA provided him with surety bonding. Today he has his own $25-million bonding ceiling. Having been selected Arizona Small Business Person of the Year in 1983, as well as National Minority Contractor of the Year by the Department of Commerce and the Department of the Interior, Ruiz is indeed a major operator and an unparalleled success story and inspiration.

The Drill Sergeant and the Woman

Can you imagine this incipient business combination: a black ex-Marine sergeant who was a construction worker and a Jewish woman who was a personnel consultant? They teamed up to form a company that drills for deep-down dirt samples in the rocky soil of New York's Manhattan, prior to construction. The ex-sergeant designed the first drill in his living room; his partner wrote the loan application and business plan. They applied to the SBA for a start-up loan and were granted $50,000. That was in 1980 when they took in $30,000 for the entire year and had to hold down outside, part-time jobs. Today, they do over a million dollars of business as Python Drilling & Testing Co., employing 16 people, mostly minorities. All this success was not accidental—the former Marine had spent his 20 years in the service working on heavy construction projects and learning all about diesel engines, and his partner had complementary skills. It is another case where technical, hands-on knowledge, joining with administrative ability and the support of a sympathetic government bureau, created a new business that has added 18 taxpayers to the American small-business community.

CRAFTS: OF BROOMS AND TEACUPS

Out of a combination of talent, ingenuity, and happenstance, a handicraft business was born and thrived. Thurman Scheumack was handicapped by a motorcycle accident, so he started a broom-making business in the Ozark foothills. But they were not ordinary brooms, and word got around. Now he produces over 20,000 a year and has an annual sales volume of $400,000; some of his creative brooms can be seen in art galleries.

In Springfield, Illinois, Ellen Matlins, a potter of some note, created a hand-painted tea set for her two little girls. By luck and design, a set came to the attention of the buyer for the prestigious toy chain, F. A. O. Schwartz. For the past two seasons, the Matlins' tea set has appeared in the company's Christmas catalog, and 500 lucky little girls are now owners of this hand-decorated collector's item. The key to catapulting your arty or craftsy talent into a profitable business is marketing.

DAY CARE FOR LATCHKEY KIDS

One of the phenomena of our current industrial age is millions of kids having no place to go after school. Both Mom and Pop are working, and families just don't have Grandma living at home, nor can they afford to pay a live-in maid. So kids have to stay overtime in kindergartens, go to a friend's house, or wander around the neighborhood with the key to their home in their pocket. To address this problem, a couple in Connecticut, both former teachers, started a day-care chain called Kidstop. But Kidstops offer more than just day care. They have well-developed learning programs, in addition to being safe after-school houses for youngsters, who may attend right up to high school. The two founders got started with a mailing campaign in various well-to-do neighborhoods, and the charges are $400 a month and up. Now they have obtained a contract from the state and have gained permission to utilize facilities in a local high school. They are looking to expand via the franchise route, using their Shelton, Connecticut, prototype as a base.

DECORATING SERVICE: CONDO COORDINATOR

In certain parts of the country, such as Florida, condominiums are the number-one choice of housing. Many buyers don't bring their northern furnishings with them. Other situations in which people start to furnish a home from scratch include immigrant buyers, first-time buyers like newly married couples, and 30- to 45-year-old single professionals, who form a large segment of this market. Into the condo-furnishing gap comes the decorator/coordinator who takes care of finding and placing the right furniture, wallpaper, knick-knacks, draperies, and pictures—in short, who does all those persnickety things that the busy or absentee owner cannot readily do for himself or herself. The coordinator may even get the utilities turned on and the deposits paid, arrange for insurance, procure extra keys, notify the post office, see that carpeting and lighting are properly installed, unpack, etc.

The condo coordinator who does it all is a relatively new service provider, and the business forms an attractive possibility for people trained in decorating, real estate, or display, or who simply have good taste. Fees range from $1000 to $2000 per job. Prospects can be found through leads from friendly decorators, condominium-sales offices, Realtors, and condo-association offices, and by advertising in newspapers, better tourist publications, and foreign-language media aimed at this market. Investment is virtually nil, though it will take some time to become profitable. Discounts obtained from vendors can be offered to clients as incentives.

EMPLOYMENT AGENCY: THREE STORIES

Tired of Retiring

It happens to tens of thousands of the elderly. They retire and try to relax: they play 18 holes of golf, make the bridge-playing circuit every day, comb the library for new novels, attend Elderhostel courses, and visit the children for the umptieth time. With enough money, they can visit exotic places or historic sites, and with a lot of money they can even start retirement businesses of their own. In the latter case, the risk element is prodigious, and we would not advise it unless there is in-depth experience in that business, at least as a lifelong hobbyist. A visit to the nearest SCORE office in order to get counseling from a fellow retiree who has entrepreneurial experience would be a good way to start.

Another possibility is to get a part-time job, which is what Bob Rheinhart of Tucson, Arizona, thought many retirees would like to do. With more than 50,000 retired people in his area, he set up Retiree Skills, Inc., a temporary employment service in which all employees are over 50 years of age. This 68-year-old ex-retiree and his crew have been responsible for putting about 800 restless individuals back to work. On his roster are over 250 local firms that love to hire elderly experts in a wide variety of fields, paying a pre-determined rate and not worrying about workmen's comp, FICA, etc. Rheinhart is ambitious, too. He's expanding into Phoenix and other nearby locations, and he's considering franchising his operation to other parts of the country. There might not be much grass growing anywhere in Tucson, Arizona, but there definitely isn't much growing under Bob Rheinhart's feet.

Filling 90 Percent of the J.O.B.S.

The trend in recent years among employment agencies has been to focus on high-paying executive placements. In these placements, the employer pays the fees, and they can go into the high five- or low six-figures. In Clearwater, Florida, Robert Norins and Steven Sokol have reversed this trend by going after the under-$25,000 employment market. They claim that this category makes up 90 percent of the labor force, but it has often been ignored by private placement firms. They formed a company called J.O.B.S. in 1982 and began to solicit employers in the area. Listings are computerized and updated daily, and applicants seeking positions are charged a $75 registration fee to use these daily listings for up to three months. This approach has been so successful that the agency has begun to franchise J.O.B.S. in other areas of the country. Since these franchise offices are tied into the main computer, applicants who wish to search for employment elsewhere must pay a modest additional fee. A J.O.B.S. franchise costs $19,500 plus the cost of setting up a business. There is a 7 percent additional royalty charge. Additional information may be obtained by writing J.O.B.S. at 3196 Gulf-to-Bay Blvd., Clearwater, FL 34619. Phone: (813) 933-6080.

Grandma the Entrepreneur

Magazines for older adults, such as *Modern Maturity*, are full of stories about retirees who got tired of retirement: They came up with an idea and went back to work—this time for themselves.

One danger in this approach is insufficient experience; such people often go into business when they have never been in business. Sometimes they invest their life's savings without knowing clearly the risks involved or realizing that they do not have the time to recoup any possible losses.

However, Pauline Black of Tulsa, Oklahoma, was one sharp lady who made a success of her retirement-age career. She started an employment service for elderly women, called Grandmothers, Inc., and now she has several offices in the area. She places over 500 of her contemporaries each month in jobs such as baby sitters, child-care supervisors, invalid companions, and new-mother helpers. It took just one ambitious lady with the appropriate vision to become a catalyst for hundreds of her peers.

EXPORTING: FIVE STORIES

Ten Things to Consider Before You Start

Whether you want to export lumber, golf clubs, used parking meters, or packaging material, the story that successful exporters tell is always the same and can be distilled down to the following rules of thumb (also see the 25 points on exporting in Chapter 9):

1. Sell only a quality product that will bring customers back and that requires little maintenance.
2. Get into export for the long haul, through declines and rises.
3. Make thorough use of available government assistance, especially in the Department of Commerce (see list of district offices).
4. Have a good distributor overseas—that is, one good one rather than a whole bunch of mediocre ones.
5. Attend as many international trade shows as time and money allow—network, network, network.

6. Look for openings for special products not available locally, even if your American wares are priced higher.

7. Take the time to learn about the laws and customs of foreign countries before you make any shipments or commitments.

8. Invest in getting professional translations of your promotional materials.

9. Explore the use and cost of telefacsimile and telex equipment to serve overseas customers rapidly.

10. Look into having an export trading company handle your overseas sales, rather than chancing your own selling.

The Sweet Fruit of Success

A decade ago, Lu Wade was trying to fill the sweet tooth of her husband Bill, while accommodating his dietary restrictions. After some experimentation, she came up with a low-sodium, low-calorie concoction composed only of pure fruit concentrates, acids, and some vegetable gum stabilizers. It tasted good, produced no allergic reactions, and seemed ideal for wider distribution to people who likewise could not tolerate dairy products. And that's how Yodolo was born.

For five years, they had produced only limited quantities of Yodolo when they went to the SCORE counselors in Spokane, Washington, for advice on how to go commercial in a larger and more profitable way. One of the first steps was exhibiting at the Pacific Northwest World Trade Exposition in Tacoma, which turned out to be the product's launching pad. The couple gave out samples of Yodolo at their booth, and the word got around like wildfire. People stood three-deep at the booth, stated Bill Wade. As a result, several distributors were signed up from other parts of the world. They signed a $1.3 million contract for the East Asian market, and the company was off and running. Prospects for domestic and international growth are bright, and an annual volume of $2 to $3 million is expected.

Sticking to Business

Making glue might sound like a simple business, but polymer chemistry is both complicated and machinery-intensive. There are glues for paper and cardboard, medical bandages, floor coverings and tiles, and fabrics. Each is different, and each is produced in big quantities in the United States. However, a polymer chemist in New Jersey discovered that in Europe there is a dearth of such manufacturing, and he decided to do something about it. A connection to a local banker brought him together with a SCORE counselor in Newark, who in turn had connections in Greece. Based on such contacts and his expertise in this science, the chemist was able to get bank loans to buy the needed machinery. After his first orders from Greece were filled, he expanded the business into Scotland, Mexico, and elsewhere. The latest gambit is a joint-venture plant in Jamaica. Favorable dollar exchange has helped, of course, but exporting American know-how is possible for an individual who knows how to use available resources and skills.

A Tuneful Tale

Michael Stoff of Southern California liked to ride a bike. It's good for you, he knew, but it also could be boring. So he developed a small, pre-Walkman stereo that could be attached to a bike and listened to while you pedaled. So far so good. The domestic market, however, was a difficult one, so Mike turned his eyes overseas, where proportionately more people ride bikes than in the United States.

Beyond having the idea, Mike had no knowledge whatsoever. He approached the local SCORE chapter and found a counselor who had had 30 years of export experience. Together, they worked out the plan that ultimately led to Tune-Totes' success. The plan included a publicity campaign mounted in overseas trade journals, attendance at international trade fairs (a list is published annually in U.S. Department of Commerce brochures), establishing overseas distributors, working with the Department of Commerce to effect letters of credit and banking transactions, and learning how to check up on foreign buyers and distributors through the Department's overseas "desks." He bought a commercial listing in the Department's *Commercial News USA*, prepared press kits in various foreign languages, and in a relatively brief period worked sales for Tune-Totes up to $1 million. That, in any language, is music to a new entrepreneur's ears.

Construction Services

Moving from Hawaii to Singapore is a mighty big jump, but Richard Heaton's Hardscapes Hawaii, Ltd. did exactly that. Hardscapes does indoor/outdoor landscaping, utilizing a synthetic hollow rock that is lightweight and easy to ship and handle. Heaton had obtained information that his services could be used in high-growth areas like Singapore and Hong Kong. However, he needed capital to expand into those foreign markets, and local banks in Hawaii were unwilling to help because Hardscapes had no collateral that assured a return on loans.

Fortunately, a member of the local SCORE chapter who was consulted had some Singapore connections. He helped Heaton set up a foreign sales corporation and attracted capital through a $1.5 million contract with Singapore builders that promised an estimated half-million dollar profit. This was the beginning, and, ultimately, Hardscapes was able to garner several million dollars worth of business—proving that even a small business can become a big success if you combine know-who and know-how.

Plant Nursery Products

Cooperation is the buzzword that created success for a number of small ornamental plant nurseries in Florida. It was doubtful that any one of them alone could expand its market overseas into the new centers of growth. But together they did it. A dozen growers organized themselves as an association, pooled knowledge and financial resources, hired a central director familiar with export promotion and management, and obtained considerable help from state and federal government resources.

As a group entity they were able to do overseas advertising; get a European greenhouse distributor; attend trade fairs in Germany, Italy, and England; and, most of all, generate sufficient sales to fill a huge container for overseas shipment. This made shipping economical and secure and showed European developers, builders, and architects that utilizing Florida-grown plants was indeed feasible. From a $2 million volume in 1985, the association is now shipping well over $12 million annually. Together they made it profitable for the individual. You might say that the association's growing is showing!

FARM ANIMAL SERVICE: A LOT OF COW SIT

You've heard of baby sitting, house sitting, and pet sitting. But have you heard of "cow sitting"? Ed and Pauli Drexler of Fabius, New York, figured that since cows need to be milked twice a day, there's a market for a cow caretaker so that Ol' McDonald can take a vacation once in a while. Is there a need for such a service? Do dairy-farm families take vacations? You bet your sweet cream they do. Even though the Drexlers' services do not come cheap—they charge at least $100 a day—the entrepreneurs have enough clients to keep the two Drexlers plus four full-time and two part-time employees busy as a cow's tail at fly time.

How do they operate? Several hours before the dairy family leaves, the Drexlers or their staff arrive to get acquainted with the bossies, write down their personal data, and generally keep them as contented as cows like to be. Recently, they have added cow sitting at cattle auctions to their line of services. This is more difficult than work on the farm, because the cows are skittish and nervous; still, the animals need to be milked, cleaned and groomed to look their best before the gavel comes down. The Drexler-trained cow sitters are now spread over six states, and the pile of customers is growing.

FASHION: TWO STORIES

Ladies' Fashions: from Big to Small

Scott Shively of Houston runs a chain of six petite fashion stores in Houston, Dallas, and Austin. He did not start with sextuplets but with a single ladies' clothing store in Houston about 10 years ago. What had prepared him for his dream goal was his job as buyer and merchandise manager of a well-known Houston department store. He found very quickly, however, that running a department or section in a large department store was very different from the scaled-down operation of a single store, where the proprietor is the chief cook and bottlewasher.

He was wise enough to realize this problem of adjustment and called for help from a SCORE counselor in Houston who had himself been the owner of two fashion stores. Together they were able to meet the special challenges involved in buying, controlling inventory, advertising, keeping accounts, hiring and training help, and keeping abreast of current fashion trends in a single proprietorship. Initially, Shively exchanged his normal 50-hour work week for 70 hours, but he was successful because he combined personal experience, outside counseling, and persistence with hard work. Today he runs six successful stores plus a seventh one that specializes in discount fashions—an outlet for his other six. Shively proved that sometimes golden acorns grow from big old oaks.

Designing Woman Discovers Fame

Half a dozen years ago a young mother with a flair for fashion design struggling to make a go in business was on the verge of giving up. A community-help organization suggested to Leslie Babbitt that she consult the local SCORE counselors in the Boston office. It proved the beginning of something big. The former general merchandise manager of famed Filene's department store, now a SCORE counselor, advised her on business operations, manufacturing, and marketing methods, and, as the point of it all, on how to make a profit. Loaded with talent and ambition, Ms. Babbitt climbed the ladder of fashion success with her line of knit designs, and in six years her gross volume rose 600 times from that of her start-up year. In November 1987, she was identified as the two-millionth client counseled by SCORE and was named "Woman of the Year" by the SBA. She has a plan for the next few years that will expand her present operation several times. Not bad for a "designing woman" who learned early and quickly that two heads are better than one.

FLOWERS: THEY MAKE MONEY GROW

There are 50,000 retail florists in the United States, and 16,000 of them are members of the FTD association. Yet, this example presents a slightly different idea: a flower subscription service. For $15 a month or $180 a year, the founder of this simple but ingenious business delivers flowers to whomever you designate. Designees range from sweethearts to business contacts. All the flowers are the same for that week's delivery so that he can take advantage of the season's best buys. Mums and carnations are generally favored as they last the best. The business can be run from home with one person on the telephone. Depending on the neighborhood and concentration of clients, up to 10 deliveries can be made per hour, the man claims. Each delivery arrives in an inexpensive bud vase with a card from the sender attached. The entrepreneur says that a single publicity article in the local paper got him started. He has been following up with small ads in the local paper and direct-mail pieces to entire office buildings. Uses he suggests for flower subscriptions are the occasions of birthdays, anniversaries, business openings, holidays like Valentine's Day and Mother's Day, illnesses and simply as reminders to your loved ones that you appreciate them.

FOOD: SIX STORIES

Do-It-Yourself Gourmet

The trend toward gourmet cooking, adventurous culinary experimentation, and fascination with foreign cuisines led Vivian Luoma to start up Home Gourmet Company in Cupertino, California. After doing some preliminary canvassing of better food stores to ascertain a market, the 39-year-old industrial psychologist and sometimes gourmet cook made arrangements with a local cooking school to use part of its premises. She brought in some students from a nearby school for the handicapped, hired two part-timers, and set to work packaging ingredients for a variety of exotic dinners.

All the dry ingredients and spices, everything except for the fresh products (meats, fresh vegetables), are packaged in little premeasured bags. Each bag contains enough for a meal to satisfy the most jaded appetites of four to six people and retails for $15 at the stores. Locally, she was able to sell the giant Safeway chain, and five outlets are added to her customer list each week—some of them through sales reps in other states. Growth was gradual and slow, but Luoma passed the break-even point last year and is planning to expand by adding a bagged line of desserts and hors d'oeuvres. Gourmet dining by the numbers is part of the national trend toward combining time-management with adventurousness in eating.

Coffee 'n' Spice, Everything Nice

From teaching in the inner city of New York to running a modest coffee-and-spice empire in Portland, Oregon, would seem like a journey of light years, but it is the true story of Mr. and Mrs. Bob Kobos. They learned how to manage people the hard way, but two years in the educational jungle of New York was sufficient. They headed to the other side of the country, their former home, with $6,000, an idea, and a well-thought-out business plan. With this they approached the local SBA for a loan under the 7(j) Program. The government loan officer was impressed with the couple's detailed research and their plan that showed both ambition and ingenuity. They received a $19,000 loan and opened a coffee, tea, and spice business. Their timing was right—gourmet products were just beginning to catch on. A friendly cabinetmaker supplied custom shelving fixtures for them in exchange for painting the couple did for him. Today, just a few years later, success is evident: the one small shop has expanded into four, featuring 20 varieties of tea, 27 varieties of coffee, and 100 different herbs and spices. A year ago they opened a wholesale division that now supplies 32 of the better restaurants in the Portland area. Sales last year went over the $2 million mark, and 45 people are on the payroll. The SBA's $19,000 investment has taken off like a rocket.

Ben & Jerry Lick Their Problems

America's third largest gourmet-ice-cream maker got its boost from a $20,000 SBA-guaranteed loan. Their own original investment was a mere $8000. A decade later, Ben & Jerry's Homemade Inc., does $30 million in sales and employs 200 people.

The setting is a small town in Vermont, where proprietors Ben Cohen and Jerry Greenfield, two big-city college dropouts from the sixties, are still amazed by their success. The Ben & Jerry's story has been told many times. Their beginning as local purveyors of premium ice cream, their rapid growth based on unique flavors that caught the attention of customers' taste buds everywhere and their family-style employee management—all spurred Ben & Jerry's success. Of course, the men's unorthodox look and way of doing business generated much publicity—something that they did not resist too much.

While their back-to-nature lifestyle and unique merchandising ideas might puzzle some people, it seems to be this very *difference* that has made their company stand out—even against the competition of Häagen Dazs (a Pillsbury company) and Frusen-Glädjé (a Kraft corporation). As far as Ben and Jerry are concerned, a lot of credit goes to their employees, most of whom they know personally, and all of whom are on a profit-sharing system based on longevity of employment. "Business has a responsibility to make the world a better place in which to live, not just to enrich yourself at the expense of others," states Jerry. It is this almost Biblical, bread-cast-upon-the-waters philosophy that has helped Ben & Jerry's lick its original small business problems.

From $4000 to $14,000 a Week

A convenience store that can show a 350 percent increase in volume in three years must be doing something right. Of course, such phenomenal growth brings problems, and they must be managed well if the owners are to avoid extending themselves beyond their personal and financial capacity. This is the story of the Wilson Convenience Store in Melrose, Massachusetts, and it's a case where timing and luck met to create opportunity.

A change from cabinet-making to running a grocery was dictated by Bob Wilson's back problem. His brother owned a property that was occupied by a convenience store whose lease was expiring. Wilson and his wife took over the property, went to the Boston SCORE chapter for counseling and guidance, and started on their road to success.

It took three months to add 1000 square feet to the existing 2500 square feet, remodel the interior, and restock with fresh merchandise. Six months later a delicatessen department was added; in another six months, there was a liquor department—which had to be separated from the main store because of a Sunday no-sale law. The following year, the couple applied for and received authorization as an agency for the state lottery. Problems like cash control, pilferage, waste, proper shelf-space allocation, vendor control, pricing control, and an inventory-ordering system were tackled one after the other. Weekly gross has risen from $4000 before they took over to $14,000 a week presently. Personal income could go to $100,000 this year. That's not just donuts 'n' coffee; that's eating caviar!

The Feel of the Fruit

Mass merchandising and prepackaging of produce through supermarkets has turned some housewives and shoppers off. One of the consistent complaints we hear about some very fine supermarkets is that they only sell prepackaged vegetables. Customers cannot tell the quality or "feel" of the produce and go to the smaller, higher-priced fruit stand or grocery (where they still can be found) to get unpackaged goods they can select individually. This trend has been noted by some fruit and vegetable dealers, like the entrepreneurial Marcellis family of St. Petersburg, Florida, and Manhattan. They are selling and delivering at least 100,000 field-grown, sun-ripened tomatoes a week—just in New York City. It's a business of the present and the future.

This Grocery Can't Go Wong

San Francisco's Haight-Ashbury area is famed for more than student uprisings. Its most enduring feature is a 32-year-old family-operated supermarket called Ashbury Market. Like so many smallish food stores these days, it is owned and managed by a family of Oriental origin—the Wongs. Jane and Walter started the business and eventually brought in Larry, Wilfred, and Arnold. Each has his assigned task: Wilfred has become the manager and resident wine expert, Larry manages the grocery end, while Arnold, still a student, runs the delicatessen department. Father Walter operates the cash register, and mother Jane handles the books. If you think this is just another hundred-thousand-dollar neighborhood grocery, think again. Last year the Wong shop grossed $2.5 million. About 50 percent of this, and the majority of the net profits, comes from the wine and deli departments. It's your typical success scenario: working hard, adapting to the times, displaying honesty in dealing with customers and with each other, and being very, very good at what they're doing. There are huge chain markets all around, most grossing more dollars, but it is doubtful that they make the kind of returns on their investment that Ashbury Market does.

FRANCHISING: LOOK BEFORE YOU LEAP

One thing that made attorney Charles Cummins a successful franchisee in San Francisco was that he did a lot of prebuying investigation. Altogether, he talked to 20 operating franchisees and five companies offering franchises. Then he chose a company, gathered some friends together who raised $120,000 among them—the cost of the franchise—and struck a deal with the Precision-Tune Auto-Repair-While-You-Wait people. After the first year of operation, Cummins' franchise grossed over $300,000. As a lawyer, Cummins had some advantages, of course. Practice in investigation and getting answers to questions, having a profession that produced income already, and knowing people who trusted him with investment capital all combined to make the deal possible.

The pluses in buying a franchise, as Cummins found out, are that the franchiser teachers you how to run the business and, because the company gets a regular percentage of your gross, continues to maintain a certain amount of interest. The result: fewer than 4 percent of franchises go bust each year, while the bankruptcy note for independently owned businesses is several times that figure; sad to say. But you still need to analyze and investigate, attend some franchise shows, talk to those already in the business as franchisees, and be prepared to work every bit as hard at running your setup as you would a nonfranchise enterprise.

GARDENING SUPPLIES

Will Raap saw an opportunity in 1984 in sales of unusual and high-quality gardening supplies throughout the United States. The only way to do it would be by mail order. Initially he tried to get an SBA-approved loan, but when he was turned down, he started anyway—driven by ambition, conviction that there were enough customers out there who appreciated better gardening products, and a business philosophy that would enable coworkers to share in any success. His Gardeners Supply Company of Burlington, Vermont, took off. From a small beginning, with moderate mailings of home-produced catalogues, the company has worked itself up to $9 million in volume, selling products costing from $5 to $5000 (the latter, sophisticated greenhouses). Raap admits to having had a certain amount of luck but also says that having "a clear focus" on his aims and "a willingness to share the rewards of success" produced the cash "that allowed relative freedom to control the destiny of our business growth without excessive outside controls." In other words, Raap's green thumb grew a business.

A GIFT-BASKET CASE THAT WAS PROFITABLE

A suburban housewife who had loads of creative ideas decided to open a gift-basket business from her home in suburban Rockville, Maryland. She made a list of themes such as special events and business openings that would lend themselves to unique gift baskets for corporate clients, business associates, key employees, etc. Then she scoured flea markets and charity stores for containers, vases, and baskets; made up illustrated flyers with sample offerings and ideas; got wholesale prices on trimmings, flowers, fruits, novelties, printing of catchy cards, delivery services, and more. Finally, she prepared lists of corporations and banks, service businesses, VIPs and professionals who could afford the $25 to $50 she would charge for her very unusual baskets and started bombarding these targets with jumbo cards.

The result: after several months, she was having fun and the requests for her product started growing and growing. To expand, she employed art students part-time from the local high school and college. The third year, she grossed nearly $100,000—selling an average of ten gift baskets a day at an average of $30 each, many of them being multiple and repeat sales.

HOME INSPECTION SERVICE TO SELLERS AND BUYERS

Home inspection was the idea of two entrepreneurs—one in the Orlando, Florida, area and the other in Pueblo, Colorado. Each service was different from the other, and yet they had similarities. The Florida business was started by a woman Realtor who simply got tired of the odd hours, weekend work, and insecurity of selling real estate. Her knowledge of what made a residence sell and her inherent good taste combined to create a presale inspection service for homeowners, giving answers and critiques to a 50-point checklist that would enhance selling their homes and obtain more money for the property. This approach allowed the woman consultant to continue working with her contacts in the real estate agencies. Solicitation of customers was through direct neighborhood fliers, real-estate-agency referrals, and classified-ad follow-ups. She operated out of her home, during daytime hours only, and required little cash except for her own maintenance.

The Pueblo start-up was by a former housing inspector who preferred to work out of an office in an "incubator" facility that offered secretarial and phone service. His presale inspections are more technical and are usually initiated by buyers, though many Realtor referrals are also received. He started with $12,000 of his own capital and after a year is beginning to show progress and profit.

INFANT AND JUVENILE ACCESSORIES

Out in Arizona, a new mother in her twenties could not afford to buy all the pretty things she wanted for the baby's room. So she made them. Friends saw her efforts and asked her to make nursery items for them, too. This gave the creative young woman the idea: Why not make a business out of what I enjoy doing? She consulted the local office of SCORE, and with the free counseling she received, she established a businesslike operation. She got other women to cut and sew the items she designed, and she started selling both to word-of-mouth customers and local stores.

Within four years she had expanded beyond nurseries to providing juvenile accessories for commercial kiddie centers and model homes, and she even had talked to a franchiser about selling out-of-town franchises to other creative women. She has attracted a number of craftspeople in the area who are making other homey, folksy accessories for nurseries, and she is planning to expand by adding manufactured items such as juvenile wallpaper and furnishings. Ambition, enthusiasm, imagination, and smarts are what helped this young woman succeed.

JEWELRY: ALL THAT GLITTERS CAN BE GOLD

There is a lot of talent lurking in the suburbs and boondocks. Some people write, some paint, some sculpt or throw pots. Others, like Brenda Hauswirth and her husband George of Salem, Oregon, design and make jewelry. For a number of years they did the work, which they loved, on a small scale, and it provided a modest living. Then they became interested in expanding, and they knew what that meant: investing more money; finding a larger working and sales location; and learning about business functions such as purchasing, inventory control, promotion, and bookkeeping.

With the advice of a retail-wise counselor from the local SCORE office, they gave up their quaint but out-of-the-way shop in an old firehouse and acquired a location near downtown Salem in a converted church building. Business doubled the first year, proving that location is a very vital ingredient in retailing. With their counselor, they created a seven-step business plan and a monthly budget and sales plan. They kept a daily record of sales and expenses, established an open-to-buy system such as department and chain stores have, maintained an inventory control book and advertising-promotion calendar, as well as an evaluation system of these efforts, and conducted a monthly review of all sales and cost figures. For a couple of artistic people this was a difficult job and quite a leap, but it paid off in increased sales, satisfaction—and profits.

JIGSAW PUZZLES

Two teachers from Dillons, Kansas, who were also trivia fans came up with a very basic idea: make learning geography fun by creating a jigsaw puzzle for the state of Kansas. After several weeks of research, they had their design and two manufacturers. The one major problem was that puzzles could only be produced in minimum quantities of 10,000 sets. That took money—$12,000 to be exact. They were able to borrow it, and within another few months the first batch rolled out of the factory. They personally sold every one, with customers ranging from a local grocery to a major school-supply house (the latter buying 5000 sets). That first year they racked up $100,000 in sales.

They went on to design puzzles for two adjacent states. By the end of 1987, they had 12 states completed and more than 80,000 puzzles sold. In another three or four years they hope to have designed jigsaw puzzles for all 50 states and approached most of the major school-supply houses. Special occasions, like state centennials, are especially good tie-ins for marketing their games. Best of all, for the Austin-Peirce Company, making money is no longer a puzzle.

KITCHEN GADGETS ON THE GO

If you're trying to locate the Weatherbee Company during the winter months, you'll find it in Harvard, Massachusetts; in the summertime, however, you'll have to go over to Martha's Vineyard, where Anne Voss and her pilot husband reside. Looking for a business that she could run out of her home while her two boys were growing up—one that did not need to be anchored to a retail location—Ann came up with inventing unique kitchen gadgets and selling them to national mail-order houses (such as Carol Wright) and to about 600 individual gourmet shops. All items she develops are contracted out for manufacture. Once manufactured, everything is entered on the home computer. Direct mail is the primary contact means for reaching the market, and a call-forwarding system keeps her available to customers. Among the

Voss items are an opening device for stubborn jars, a recipe-holding easel, a measurements converter, and a slide rule that "dials" cooking ingredients. Thus far, the Vosses are a relaxed and successful home-business couple, enjoying the best of both worlds—making money as they go, so to speak.

LOANS: A FRIEND CALLED MOHED

While these success stories are a collection of private enterprise achievements, there is a city bureaucratic entity that is worth mentioning—and even emulating by other municipalities. Dianne Feinstein, the very visible mayor of San Francisco, has been the spark plug behind a department called MOHED—the Mayor's Office of Housing and Economic Development. Bill Witte and Sue Lee are two of the staff of expert ombudspeople who help new businesses and old ones get through bureaucratic red tape. Need information about zoning? About suitable lease or real estate purchase? Wonder who to see about a municipal license? Want to finance a proven expansion? Calling MOHED is most likely to yield results.

The Small Business Loan Program is one of MOHED's sections that has been exceptionally helpful. Larger, fixed-asset financing programs also have been put into motion to help relocate and expand a variety of businesses, including Merchandising Methods, a mailing firm; Hoefer Scientific, a medical instrument maker; Applied Dielectrics, a circuit manufacturer; MJB Building, which now houses a number of endangered printing companies; 1550 Bryant, a light industrial condominium that is an incubator for minority-owned businesses; and Flying Salmon, the first retail outlet developed by a Japanese fish cannery. And the list goes on. No wonder so many businesses, as well as visitors, have "left their hearts in San Francisco"!

MERCHANDISING: THREE STORIES

Gypsy Marketing

A temporary-retailing phenomenon has surfaced in areas like Miami and New York. It is a here-today-gone-tomorrow approach that takes advantage of desirable store locations that happen to be temporarily vacant. First the sharp entrepreneur canvasses high-traffic locations, either downtown or in a shopping center or shopping strip, and finds a site. Then he or she contacts the owner or Realtor and offers a reasonable rent, with the understanding that the premises may be occupied by someone who will leave within a couple of months. The deal is concluded—this way, the owner gets some rent out of it while the store would otherwise stand empty—and the "gypsy marketer" moves in. The merchandise is usually distress goods, bought cheaply or taken in on consignment (to be paid for only when actually sold). A big banner goes up overhead that proclaims "Grand Opening Sale," just as a month or two or three later, another sign will go up that reads "Going Out of Business Sale." (These are two irresistible occasions to people looking for bargains.) Enticements such as outside sandwich signs, reading "Discontinued Merchandise" or "Last Chance," balloons, and clowns are some of the promotional tools used. These temporary storekeepers can make a fortune, and it doesn't take a crystal ball to see how it's done. All you need is strength, guts, and the soul of a gypsy.

Surplus Produces $urplu$

This form of merchandising can be a very lucrative business, but it's also a tricky one. First, you, the dealer, buy what's called distress or surplus merchandise—either from a manufacturer who wants to get rid of it at the end of a season, or at an auction, or from a business that's gone bankrupt. Then you find a buyer, perhaps a chain store or an exporter, who'll buy the whole shebang at a profit. Or, you open a store on a short-term lease, or go into a bunch of flea markets and sell the surplus merchandise piecemeal at a whopping profit. Both approaches have been immensely profitable—although it must be said in all honesty, that we know of as many disasters as successes. It depends on how favorably you buy and on how fast you turn over your goods—that is, on having good resale connections.

You also can act as a broker or go-between: line up a customer before you conclude the purchase and then have the merchandise shipped as one bulk entity directly to the purchaser. In that case, you never touch the wares; you merely facilitate their exchange. The latter scenario is more likely with industrial goods than with consumer merchandise. It's a neat method and might bring a 5 to 10 percent profit; on the other hand, the piecemeal, resale approach could bring profits of several hundred percent—with the attendant risk of losing your shirt. This is not a business for the innocent; it's for the horse trader—the sharp merchandiser, promoter, and speculator. One man we know makes six figures a year, but don't say we didn't tell you about the caveats.

Mobile Selling

The "pushcart brigade" has become a national merchandising phenomenon. Not long ago, the prestigious International Council of Shopping Centers, representing shopping-center entrepreneurs, held its first Temporary Tenant Conference. It was a sign that kiosk concessionaires have become a recognized retail force in America. Not that all of these "temps" are small, however. Gail Bird of Boston has been a pushcart lady for a dozen years at the renowned Rouse emporium located at Faneuil Hall. By her own admission she has grossed as much as a quarter of a million dollars in a single year, selling novelties, souvenirs, jewelry, etc.—in a space not much larger than a queen-sized bed.

For a small retailer wanting to go into business, this is indeed an opportunity worth investigating. The space might be only four by six feet, but this 24 square feet, or a little more, can cost from $100 to $250 a week, or $430 to $1100 per month. That's $216 to $552 per square foot on an annualized basis—far, far more than ordinary retailers pay even on Rodeo Drive or Fifth Avenue. And you still have to negotiate a favorable lease with management (10 to 15 percent of gross sales should be tops).

Still, it is an opportunity for the minimerchandiser to get into a business of his or her own. Shopping malls, hotel lobbies, airports, fairs, and some city sidewalks are all locations where such mobile "temp tycoons" can set up shop. The hours are long, the pace tiring, and an outgoing personality is required to attract buyers and make sales. But it's a great way to set your own pace. You can also sell much of your own merchandise and make a whopping profit. Your initial risk is $1000 to $5000. Reading *Cart Your Way to Success* ($19.95) is a good first investment. Get it from Birdhouse Enterprises, 110 Jennings Ave., Patchogue, NY 11772.

MOTEL OWNER

No matter what business you are in or plan to get into, cash flow is a very necessary aspect. If it stops, it's like having the blood coursing through your veins suddenly encounter a clot. That blockage could kill you in very short order.

A motel owner in the Southwest was doing very well with a franchised facility. He was, in fact, doing too well. It took more cash than he had available to meet increased operating and maintenance expenses. His mandatory monthly payments were choking him. With the help of a local SCORE ex-banker, he applied to several local banks for an interim loan—five of them to be exact.

Nothing was happening, and finally the motel owner went to the Small Business Administration. The loan officer there considered the appeal valid and worked with one of the banks to make the man's 15-year-loan application a reality. The entrepreneur was thus able to consolidate his debts, reduce his annual debt service by $2000, and continue to grow in an otherwise healthy business.

PACKAGING: DESIGNING A BETTER CARTON

When you're already in your 50s, starting a new business becomes a little more difficult. You've got the experience and patience, contacts, and perhaps a little money saved up, but you don't have the time and the personal elasticity. Still, the entrepreneurial dream is a strong one no matter what the age. Chuck and Sue Olsen of Keokuk, Iowa, had all the pluses and more. After 30 years with a carton manufacturing company, Chuck yearned to be in business for himself, and he finally came to the conclusion that it's now or never. Armed with a unique design for a better carton and a few customer contacts, he approached a local banker for advice and financing.

The latter suggested that the couple call in the local SCORE counselors, and together they made up the business plan, evaluated the new product, established its potential for sales, determined manufacturing space requirements, established machinery costs, and determined the kind and number of employees needed. Both the local bank and the city community loan program advanced financing. Within a couple of years, the Keokuk Korrugated Karton Kompany not only was off and running but doing a million dollars a year. More than two dozen employees are now on the payroll—proving that even after middle age, dreams can come true if you have the skills, determination, and a better mousetrap.

PETS: CRITTER SITTER SERVICE

Taking care of pets is sometimes as important as baby sitting, because pet owners often regard their four-legged loves as their children. Patti Morgan of North Carolina has made pet sitting, which involves staying in people's houses to care for the animals, into a serious profession. She not only runs a regular employment service for pet sitters, but she has written a book about it (*Pet Sitting for Profit*, $9.95, can be ordered from New Beginnings Publications, P.O. Box 540, Pinnacle, NC 27043). She gets reliable help from contacts in local humane societies and similar organizations. And, Ms. Morgan asserts, it is not a cash-intensive business so not hard to get into: "It doesn't take much money to start a pet-sitting service, and there's no inventory to maintain." Even vets are prospects for referrals, because some of the animal doctors would rather not board their charges. Within a three-year period, the Morgan enterprise has grown to include 30 part-time sitters. The dogs, cats, and more exotic animals are happy, too, because now they can remain in their own habitats and do not need to be tranquilized in strange and often cramped cages.

PICKLES

Some success stories don't get written overnight. For Carl Hall of Atkins, Arkansas, it took more than twenty years. Hall owns the Atkins Pickle Company but he didn't acquire financial control over the then 20-year-old company till 1964. What enabled him to do this was a $700,000 loan from the SBA. The latter believed that Hall could provide employment for more people than the then-present owners, and he came through with flying colors. From 100 employees and less than a million dollars in sales, he made the company a $20 million pickle business with 400 employees. It has become the largest cucumber buyer in a three-state area, thus creating a lot of secondary employment.

Quality and persistence have paid off for the company. One of the reasons for success has been the fact that the company only processes the very best pickles—"the Cadillacs of the pickle industry," according to Hall. Hall sold his interest six years ago when he was 83, but it is still one of the three top pickle packers in America and the largest employer in his area. As many as 2000 people depend on the fortunes of the Atkins Pickle Company, and they sure relish it.

PUBLISHING "CELEBRITY"

Ever since the movie *Front Page* appeared, journalism has been one of the professions that young men and women dream about. Financial empires have been built by Hearst, Newhouse, Gannett, Condé Nast, Strauss, Ochs, Graham, Simon and Schuster, and many more. It is still possible to start a new publication, and thousands answer the siren call each year. One of them was Douglas J. Dobbs. He was an actor with Disneyworld, when he and his young wife got their idea in 1987. There were many young, aspiring, unemployed performers who might want to use an economical, widely distributed advertising vehicle. With the counsel of a friend in the newspaper business, he scraped together $10,000 in savings and made up a "dummy." In his spare time he contacted advertising prospects—other actors and entertainers—as well as printing resources and distributors. Within three months he was ready, and, with his wife's assistance in writing, proofreading, telephoning, ad preparation, and billing, he issued Vol. I, No. 1 of "Celebrity," his slick, eight-page talent newspaper. Doug Dobbs is still publishing regularly each month, and hundreds of talented performers are getting into the limelight as a result. He works two jobs, it's true, but when you're young, energetic, and just a little hungry, hard work is not an obstacle.

REFERRAL SERVICE

For a long time acquaintances and friends used to call Colette Feinberg for advice and referrals. She was a management consultant and people expected her to know who was good at what. Finally she and her husband, Sander, started a business called Service Referrals Unlimited. To keep overhead down and make work more convenient for them, they operated out of their home.

They solicited 160 providers or suppliers who were willing to pay $150 a year to be on the Feinbergs' recommended list of services. Then they advertised and spread the word that they would take clients, who would pay either $5 per referral or $50 per year for unlimited referrals. They had a good response that proved there were lots of people who liked the idea of being able to get the name of a good accountant, doctor, caterer, handyman, or whatever by calling SRU 24 hours a day (after hours an answering machine would take the message for the next day's call-back). The advantage of this business is that it requires little up-front investment and can be operated from home. The disadvantage is that it might take a long time to get going.

RESTAURANT START-UP

There are probably more restaurants opened in any one year than any other kind of new business. Also, there are probably more restaurants that close in any one year than any other kind of business. Major American cities, especially those that get heavy tourism, might have 1000 to 2000 eateries competing with each other. Road patterns, changing tastes, a single well-publicized goof, a shift in politics in a foreign land—all of these can affect the fortunes of a restaurant. Happily, the American public is eating out in greater and greater numbers. The discovery of ethnic cuisines and the unending popularity and types of fast-food places add to the growth of this industry in America.

The national accounting firm of Horwath & Laventhol has issued a primer that offers five helpful hints for start-up entrepreneurs: (1) target your location to the clientele you will be serving; (2) don't sign a gross percentage lease, for it can break you; (3) pay most attention to the design and equipment of the kitchen; (4) do a daily check of all costs, since the waste in a restaurant operation is prodigious, as is thievery; (5) good service by well-trained personnel is as important as tasty food, often even more so. Bon appetit!

A discussion of restaurant successes and failures requires an entire book, but here we can only pinpoint the reasons for one success. The business is the Kaffee Klatsch, located in a Cincinnati shopping mall and operated by a Mr. and Mrs. Schmidt. It is successful and was successful almost from the day they drew the first cup of coffee out of the shiny new urn. But there's more to the story.

First of all, the Schmidts had both worked in restaurants in various capacities, including management. While they wanted to open a place of their own, they did not know a great deal about the actual business operation of a restaurant. They picked a store-front location near their home to make things convenient. Fortunately, the next step they took was to seek counsel at the local SCORE office, where a member who had been a food corporation executive steered them into approaching their projected new business in a careful and scientific manner. The storefront proved to be the wrong location: there was little food traffic, inadequate parking, restrictions on signs, little likelihood of neighborhood acceptance. Had they opened there, they would have gone bankrupt in a short time and lost most of their life's savings. Many surveys and contacts later, the right location was found, an acceptable lease worked out, and style and fixturing determined. A bank loan was even arranged. The opening and first year were a smashing success, because the Schmidts did their homework.

ROOMMATE-FINDING SERVICE

In many parts of the country roommate-finding services are popular, especially where you have a large number of young professionals and students. In Nashville, Tennessee, Denise Walker started Roommate Referral Service that is now a successful money-maker. The business was born out of necessity. Then it was tried, tested, and refined, and now it includes the following ingredients: (1) screening and interviewing potential roommates before trying to team them up; (2) a $37.50 fee for those searching for a roommate; (3) an $8 fee for those seeking to share a room or home; (4) a $29.50 fee when the seeker has successfully found a home or room; (5) a home-sharing lease agreement that spells out the rules and protects both parties; (6) a one-month trial period to make sure the match is compatible to both parties and a rematch if it is not.

Sometimes matches are made between young men and women, with the understanding that this is a platonic business arrangement. Most of the clients are single, middle-class people between 23 and 35. Promotion consists primarily of notices to new tenants in apartment complexes, classified ads in newspapers, a listing in the Yellow Pages, posters on bulletin boards, and, of course, word of mouth.

SECRETARIAL SERVICE AT SIXTY

When you're in your 50s or even 60s and your company folds up or you get dismissed, it's tough. But not impossible. Nancy Miller had good solid experience with an engineering firm and she wasn't about to fold up her tent and steal away to a nursing home. She started a business providing secretarial help to engineering firms, included microfilming records—a service she had found very necessary in that profession. Her advice to would-be entrepreneurs is to go ahead and follow your instincts and experience. The requirements, she says, are that you have a good knowledge of the business, have a few customers lined up ahead of time (or at least have friendly connections with some), and lean on as many people as possible who can give you professional advice.

Only three days after leaving her old job, Miss Miller began working on her own enterprise, and one of the first contacts she made was with the local SCORE office. Two of the volunteer counselors gave her exactly the help and encouragement she needed, especially in an area in which she was weak—bookkeeping and accounting. Starting small in a 250-square-foot rented space, she had worked herself up into her own 3600-square-foot building, with four full-time and four part-time employees. It took eight years to do this and it took a lot of self-confidence and smarts, but if you have both, success is probably just around the corner.

SHOE MANUFACTURING: THE REEBOK STORY

This is not so much a primer on how to start a $1.2 billion shoe-manufacturing business, as it is an inspiring story about one man's success. Throughout the seventies Paul Fireman worked as a distributor for a rather obscure British running-shoe manufacturer called Reebok. During this period, Nike, Adidas, Head, and other athletic-footwear giants monopolized the athletic shoe market.

In 1981, Fireman noted the increasing popularity of aerobics. He talked to some aerobics instructors and learned that the men and women who participated in this combination of calisthenics and dancing did so either in ordinary sneakers, ballet shoes, or even barefoot. All that bouncing was tough on the feet, and Fireman planned to make it easier. He created a leather-body shoe with a soft, rubber sole and a lot of foot support built in. By 1982 he was ready for the market, and the Reebok exercise shoe took its leap. His powerhouse competitors required two years to enter the race, and by that time Fireman and his Reeboks were ruling the aerobic trade—and were on their way to grossing over a billion dollars a year. Once Fireman perceived an opening in the market, he did his homework, took the necessary risk—calculated on pragmatic evidence and experience—and became famous. We thought that you would get a kick out of this story.

SUMMER CAMPS

A couple in Maryland, both former teachers, started a sports-and-crafts-oriented summer camp. They ran it for a dozen years, making a nice year-round living from it, and then sold it at a whopping profit. Another couple—he a museum curator, she a working artist—established an arts-oriented camp on a lake in Maine. They employed professional artists and a ballerina to teach ballet. Like their Maryland counterparts, this couple ran the enterprise profitably for a dozen years and then sold it for a big, six-figure sum.

Running a camp is only a full-time occupation during the summer months. However, it can require part-time activity the rest of the year to do the following: line up young customers; make presentations before groups and associations; do the advertising and promotion; mail out answers to inquiries; and arrange for the programs, food service, insurance, health care, and general maintenance of the property. It does take considerable up-front investment that first year, but many specialty camps today charge upward of $1000 a month for taking care of little Nellie or Lewis, and gross annual income can go well over $100,000. Keep in mind that more and more specialty camps, including those for adults and senior citizens, are being established—featuring self-improvement, yoga, weight control, music, writing, and other recreation and education-oriented themes.

TABLE DECORATING

Here's the typical scenario: A young or not-so-young mother lives in a suburban home with a double garage and a recreation room, a professional husband with a decent income but a demanding schedule, and an ambition bursting to escape from its confines. The typical solution is a business that can be conducted from home while mother can keep an eye on the children. It also has to be one that can be operated without too much outside help and can be started with a small amount of seed money. And that's how Lois's table-decorating business was born six years ago. It wasn't as easy as it may sound. Many classes were taken in flower and balloon decorating, table setting, and color coordination. There were days spent hunting down resources, shopping in established stores, contacting caterers and party halls, and thinking about how to publicize the enterprise—word-of-mouth, the most solid method of attracting customers, is a slow process.

Home businesses have their disadvantages, of course, and the worst are being on call 24 hours a day, having to give more service than a store or office business, and worrying about the zoning inspector. Another headache is that working out of a home brings out the bargain-hunting clients—because you have a low overhead, they feel they can haggle over the price. And then there is the problem of getting help. At first the older kids' school friends come by and make a few bucks, but pretty soon they tire of the pressure and disappear. Just train new ones and hope for the best. Six years later, Lois's business is going strong and even growing. But working from home is not all roses.

WINDOWS TO SUCCESS

It is easy to see that Window Headquarters in Brooklyn, New York, is a successful small business. But then any company that starts up a manufacturing plant and within one year tops a million dollars, must be doing something right. It wasn't really easy or simple, according to partners Michael Verstanding and his brothers-in-law Daniel and David Malek. The group had a decade of experience working for others in the window manufacturing business. Now they were going into business for themselves and needed money for a start-up. After contacting three banks and being turned down by all of them, one of the partners suggested, "Let's talk to the SCORE people. What do we have to lose?"

They did and they won. The local business counselors, whose services are free, started the new entrepreneurs at the beginning: They said develop a business plan, and take this to the bank with the loan application. They also advised writing to all possible prospective customers to elicit some commitment for the new company's better and cheaper products, organizing an efficient production line for manufacturing, and planning to give the time-consuming and vulnerable installation process out to subcontractors. This is exactly what the trio did—and the very first banker okayed a loan for $80,000 based on the business plan and the letters received from prospective customers. Yes, it's clear to see that proper preparation is the window to success.

WRITING: AUTHOR! AUTHOR!

Each year 500,000 would-be authors hopefully send off their manuscripts to hundreds of publishers or, in some cases, to literary agents. Hardly 10 percent get beyond the first reading on the other end and have a chance of being published. Would-be authors come in all sizes, shapes, ages, races, religions, and colors. It matters little whether you are a pauper or a millionaire. It's hard to break into that rarefied circle of published writers unless you want to invest $3000 to $10,000 and publish your creative output yourself. There's nothing wrong with the latter. Having a book, neatly bound, titled, and bearing your name across the title page, can give you more satisfaction than spending a comparable heap of dollars on a vacation trip. However, actually having your work accepted by an agent and a publisher, getting that first advance check, and being referred to as an author when introduced—why, the feeling from that can hardly be valued in money.

How do you get there? Networking is one way, because it is a little surer than trusting to luck. It happened to this writer. As a former public relations director of a national organization, I was called for some information by a local writer. Pretty soon we met to continue the question-and-answer game. During this process I asked him the name of his agent, and then I contacted that person with an idea and an outline for a proposed book. Because I came recommended, the proposal was accepted, and within three weeks I had a positive response from a prominent national publisher—John Wiley & Sons. Networking did it. Know-who and know-how working together. In that order.

Part Three

Resources

SELECTED SMALL BUSINESS BOOK LIST

Libraries and bookstores are full of information on business. There are paperbacks, hardbacks, reference directories, and even tapes and video programs—not to mention magazines galore, newsletters, and newspaper business sections. To help further, there are indexes issued monthly that tell you what magazine articles were published on business subjects, and the information librarian can lead you to fact files brimming with business information clippings. Besides public libraries, there are business and association libraries; corporate libraries, libraries kept at chambers of commerce, Small Business Administration offices, and at information departments at federal and state agencies such as Labor, Agriculture, Commerce, and Interior; and don't forget the many libraries at universities and colleges. Surely, there is no dearth of information sources for the businessperson—whether you are just starting up, want to expand your operation, or have run into trouble and want to try and help yourself first. The following is a selection of 50-plus books published in recent years. They can whet your whet your appetite to dig deeper and help you on the road to success and profit.

Alarid, William, and Gustav Berle. *Free Help from Uncle Sam.* Puma Publishing Co., 1670 Coral Dr., Santa Maria, CA 93454, 1989.

This reference book gives lists and descriptions of the myriad of government bureaus in Washington and elsewhere in the United States that offer information and financial assistance. It is a well-organized, indexed guide through the multibillion-dollar maze of help that is available to the businessperson—usually for free. Includes a selection of actual success stories by small entrepreneurs, most having had help from a government entity.

Alston, Frank M., Margaret M. Worthington, and Louis P. Goldsman. *Contracting with the Federal Government.* New York: John Wiley & Sons, Inc., 2d ed., 1988.

This expensive volume, 8½" × 11" in size, 527 pages, was produced by the prestigious international accounting firm, Price Waterhouse. It details tested ways to conduct business smoothly and profitably with the world's largest buyer—the federal government. Topics include new government regulations and requirements, equitable adjustments, terminations, audit reviews, and disputes. Especially useful to your accountant—crammed with information and forms.

Bangs, David H., Jr. *The Business Planning Guide: Creating a Plan for Success in Your Own Business.* Upstart Publishing Co., 12 Portland St., Dover, NH 03820, 1988. Also available in Spanish as *La Guia del Plan de Negócios.*

This is an updated version of the first edition that sold 150,000 copies. Used by many SCORE chapters as a planning aid, it includes plenty of samples and worksheets, as well as a good business plan and financing proposal.

Christensen, Kathy. *Women and Home-based Work.* New York: Henry Holt, 1988.

The author, a professor of psychology at New York University, conducted a survey among 7000 women who work at home, The results, should *you* plan to work at home, will astound you. This book reveals the truth about child-care help, computer usage, hours actually worked, loneliness, isolation, and earnings. Twenty in-depth interviews with women home-workers are included.

Connor, Richard A., Jr., and Jeffrey P. Davidson. *Getting New Clients.* New York: John Wiley & Sons, Inc., 1987.

The authors list numerous, tested techniques of acquiring new clients and maintaining current ones. Topics include planning and conducting effective business discussions with the right contact, identifying unmet or poorly met needs of prospective clients, preparing a mailing of response-getting contact packages, and working in the way that is most productive for you.

Connor, Richard A., Jr., and Jeffrey P. Davidson. *Marketing Your Consulting and Professional Services.* New York: John Wiley & Sons, Inc., 1985.

This thoroughly practical book targets the marketing techniques needed to produce optimum revenue. Methods included are selling in person, using direct mail, advertising, writing brochures, and getting free publicity in the local press. Can be used as a step-by-step guide for almost any service business.

Cornish, Clive G. *Basic Accounting for the Small Business.* TAB Books, Blue Ridge Summit, PA 17214, 1988.

A compact and handy paperback that every small entrepreneur should become acquainted with—unless you have taken a basic accounting course in college, which most of us haven't.

Also from TAB Books:
Coltman, Michael M. *Buying and Selling a Small Business,* 1988.
Halloran, James W. *The Entrepreneur's Guide to Starting a Successful Business,* 1988.
Paulsen, Timothy. *Collection Techniques for the Small Business,* 1988.
Roberson, Cliff. *The Businessperson's Legal Advisor,* 1988.

Davidson, Jeffrey P. *Avoiding the Pitfalls of Starting Your Own Business.* New York: Walker and Co., 1988.

The biggest pitfall for an entrepreneur is an unrealistic attitude about what can be accomplished and when, according to this author. He advises tripling the expected length of time to reach a projected goal and doubling the amount for expenses. While this book is not intended as a brake on small-business start-ups, it does substitute realism for wishful thinking.

Davidson, Jeffrey P. *Marketing on a Shoestring*. New York: John Wiley & Sons, Inc., 1988.

This book offers many tips for marketing your product or services using vehicles beyond the costly, traditional ones that small start-ups can rarely afford. It covers such topics as telemarketing; attracting reliable, low-cost personnel; meeting lots of prospects inexpensively; and getting the biggest bang for your advertising buck.

Delaney, Robert, Jr., and Robert Howell. *How to Prepare an Effective Business Plan*. New York: AMACOM, 1989.

This spiral-bound book is an excellent step-by-step manual on completing a workable business plan. It includes charts, forms, and graphs. (There is a 10 percent discount for American Management Association members.)

Delaney, William A. *So You Want to Start a Business!* New York: Prentice-Hall, 1984.

This remarkably candid treatment is still good reading. Mentions countless real-life experiences including both successes and failures; points out repeatedly that in this country anyone can shoot for the moon—and either make it or fall flat on his or her face. The author is especially good in detailing ways of working with the U.S. Government.

Diamond, Michael R., and Julie L. Williams. *How to Incorporate*. New York: John Wiley & Sons, Inc., 1987.

This is a handbook for entrepreneurs and professionals who have decided to incorporate themselves and/or their businesses. Shows you how to maximize the benefits of incorporation and avoid pitfalls that exist when you add "Inc." to your business name, what forms you need, when to use subchapter S incorporation, and how to reduce your company's tax exposure.

Estes, Sherrill Y. *Selling Power: Sell Like a Pro!* Acropolis Books, 2400 17th St., NW, Washington, DC 20009, 1988.

While selling is a highly skilled and profitable profession, 90 percent of those who start drop out after a while. This book explains why this happens and tells how to avoid the pitfall. Gives basic steps to successful selling, pointers on how to become an expert consultant, and tips on closing and getting the order. The author conducts more than 100 sales seminars a year.

Ewing, S. D., and C. H. Maloney. *Minority Capital Resource Handbook.* Securities Industry Minority Capital Formation, L'Enfant Plaza East, SW, Washington, DC 20024, 1987.

A small, realistic guide to raising capital for minority entrepreneurs, this handbook outlines ways of finding and dealing with intermediaries, advisers, and venture capitalists. Gives six points to consider when making a proposal and includes a sample proposal.

Fine, Seymour H., and Raymond Dreyfack. *Customers: How to Get Them, How to Serve Them, How to Keep Them.* Chicago: Dartnell, 1988.

This 300-page, three-ring binder workbook tackles the all-important topic of customer satisfaction. It is a first-rate guide that simplifies its presentations with numbered paragraphs. Included are the six surprising ways a smaller firm holds the advantage over larger companies.

Foster, Dennis. *Franchising for Free.* New York: John Wiley & Sons, Inc., 1988.

While the cost of some franchises can go into the six-figure range, this author claims that there are at least six ways to finance a franchise without using your own money. He offers criteria to help you decide which franchise is best for you, lists 250 franchisers, and tells how to contact potential financial backers.

Foster, Dennis L. *The Rating Guide to Franchises.* New York: Facts on File, 1988.

More than 800,000 Americans own and operate franchises. If you are planning to acquire one, this book will be the impartial consumers' guide you need for an informed decision. It steers you through the jungle of statistics and legalese, giving direct and hidden costs, litigation records, and opinions of present franchisees.

General Business Services. *Tax Tips for the Small Business Owner and Professional.* Annual publication of General Business Services, 20271 Goldenrod La., Germantown, MD 20874-4090.

Updated annually, this comprehensive collection of tax-saving and planning ideas includes tax charts and worksheets.

Goldstein, Jerome. *How to Start a Family Business and Make It Work.* "In Business" Magazine, Box 323, Emmaus, PA 18049.

Choosing a business, assessing your family members' skills, internal financing, and survival are covered in this practical guide.

Goldstein, Harvey A. *Up Your Cash Flow.* Granville Publications, 10960 Wilshire Blvd., Los Angeles, CA 90024, 1988.

If the premise of the book is accurate, then the advice of this author, a CPA, could increase your profits by 25 to 50 percent. The book explains how to cut overhead, monitor income and outgo, prepare a next-year's forecast, and get your bank's loan officer to say "okay." It is valuable primarily for existing businesses.

Kamoroff, Bernard. *Small-Time Operator: How to Start Your Own Small Business.* Bell Springs Publishing, P.O. Box 640, Laytonville, CA 95454, 1987.

This manual was written by a CPA, which explains why you will find an emphasis on tax problems and laws, as well as a 43-page addendum of ledgers and worksheets. Considering that it *was* written by an accountant, it is remarkably readable and helpful. A bonus is the author's sense of humor, while the illustrations add considerable frosting to the presentation.

Klueger, Robert. *Buying and Selling a Business: A Step-By-Step Guide.* New York: John Wiley & Sons, Inc., 1988.

Treats the subject from both sides and from alpha to omega. The book attempts to match criteria to your talents, lifestyle, and personality; gives pointers for negotiating, financing, and closing the deal. The text will help you evaluate a business when buying, as well as maximize its value when selling.

J. K. Lasser Tax Institute. *How to Run a Small Business.* New York: McGraw-Hill Book Co., 1988.

This is the fifth edition of the venerable organization's classic guide. It covers the whole gamut of small business subjects: taxes, finances, computerization, employee theft, credit, mail-order selling, and more.

Laurance, Robert. *Going Freelance: A Guide for Professionals.* New York: John Wiley & Sons, Inc., 1988.

The author provides artists, advertising people, consultants, and 122 other categories of self-employed professionals with a valuable resource directory of 125 professional freelance organizations, networks, and support groups. The book tells how to sell your freelance services and how to get tax benefits from doing so. Includes a chapter on the life-style changes that many people overlook or fail to anticipate before they make the decision to go it alone.

Lele, Milind M., and Jagdish N. Sheth. *The Customer Is Key.* New York: John Wiley & Sons, Inc., 1987.

Do you want your customers to buy more? Pay a premium for your product? Stick with you through good times and bad? This book advises making your customer king and offers techniques in product design, manufacturing, sales, distribution, and after-sales. It is especially pertinent for vendors of quality wares and American products that are buffeted by cheap-labor-market imports.

Leslie, Mary, and David D. Seltz. *New Businesses Women Can Start and Successfully Operate.* Farnsworth Publishing Co., Rockville Center, NY 11570, 1987.

This women's guide to financial independence is organized in 12 sections and discusses more than 100 different businesses.

Liebers, Arthur. *How to Start a Profitable Retirement Business.* Pilot Books, 103 Cooper St., Babylon, NY 11702, 1975.

Explains what you should know *before* you decide to get into a business of your own. This lean, compact little volume touches on home businesses, part-time business, and those that can be started up for under $1000.

Also from Pilot Books:
Harmon, Charlotte. *The Flea Market Entrepreneur*, 1975.
Mangold, M. A. *How to Buy a Small Business*, 1975.
Null, Gary. *Profitable Part-Time, Home-Based Businesses*, 1975.
Small, Samuel. *Starting a Small Business After 50*, 1975.

McVicar, Marjorie, and Julia F. Craig. *Minding My Own Business: Entrepreneurial Women Share Their Secrets for Success.* Richard Market Publishers, Inc., 200 Madison Ave., New York, NY 10016.

Using the experience of more than 100 women business owners, this slim book gives start-up and operating information tailored to women entrepreneurs. Offers details on retail, service, and manufacturing businesses; includes reference material.

Merrill, Ronald E., and Henry D. Sedgwick. *The New Venture Handbook.* AMACOM, New York: 1988.

Here is everything you need to know to start and run your own business, say the authors. The book offers research, business plan, timing, eclectic money sources, and numerous real-life examples. Some unusual situations are discussed, such as the case of high profits leading to bankruptcy.

Miller, Peter G. *Media Marketing: How to Get Your Name and Story in Print and on the Air.* New York: Harper & Row, 1987.

Taking advantage of opportunities for free publicity is one of the frequently overlooked methods of promoting your business and products. This book tells you how to go about maximizing this technique. It contains a great deal of how-to information to back up its claims.

Mucciolo, Louis. *Make It Yours! How to Own Your Own Business.* New York: John Wiley & Sons, Inc., 1987.

There are three principal ways to acquire a business of your own: buy one, start one from scratch, or buy a franchise. The author presents pros and cons of each and cites specific examples of successful entrepreneurs.

Nicholas, Ted. *How to Form Your Own Corporation without a Lawyer for under $50.* Enterprise Publishers, 725 Market St., Wilmington, DE 19801, 1987.

The sale of nearly 900,000 copies of this book, mostly by mail, seems to indicate that success can be achieved just by writing the right book. But this volume tells you how it was done as well as offering hints, forms, step-by-step instructions, and wisdom on how to minimize your tax bite. Needless to say, this advice has made a millionaire of the author.

Oasis Press. *Starting and Operating a Business in (State).* Oasis Press, 300 North Valley Drive, Grants Pass, OR 97526.

Expert advice and all essential facts needed to start a new business are contained in 51 individual binders, for each of the 50 states plus the District of Columbia. There is a basic binder, and you can order one or as many individual state binders as you wish. The authors of these informative chapters are local attorneys, CPAs, educators, and business people. Nontechnical explanations of state laws, taxes, and regulations affecting business in that state will save you a great deal of running around. Each supplement includes worksheets and checklists. Orders may be phoned in, toll free, on 1-800-228-2275 with a credit card.

Olsen, Nancy. *Starting a Mini-Business: A Guidebook for Seniors.* Fair Oaks Publications, Sunnyvale, CA 94086, 1987.

This is a large paperback with large print, designed and written for re-tirees who changed their minds—and now want to explore starting a small business of their own. It's a step-by-step guide to low-risk, part-time businesses that can most likely be operated from home.

Pring, Roger. *The Instant Business Forms Book.* New York: John Wiley & Sons, Inc., 1987.

This book probably contains every form—over 200 of them—that you will ever need in business. They are ready for copying and are even perforated for easy removal. Each is printed on 8½" × 11" high-opacity paper and designed so that they can be folded to fit into a window envelope for mailing.

Smith, Allan H. *Business for Profits*. Success Publishing Co., 10258 Riverside Dr., Palm Beach Gardens, FL 33410, 1987.

The author promises 25 money-making secrets in addition to a lot of good, basic information. Topics include how to choose the right business, making up a workable business plan, finding and motivating employees, controlling dishonesty, and avoiding common mistakes. The author and his wife Judy have found a way of combining entrepreneurship with living in their own little paradise—certainly a pragmatic recommendation for this book.

Smith, G.N., and P.B. Brown. *Sweat Equity*. New York: Simon & Schuster, 1986.

How-they-did-it stories from the founders and leaders of 150 of America's best growth companies. Stimulating information will be an inspiration to start-up entrepreneurs.

Stern, Howard H. *Running Your Own Business*. New York: Crown Publishers, Inc., 1988.

This paperback handbook of facts and information functions as a primer. It covers a great many basic points and is introduced by Laurence J. Peter, the author of *The Peter Principle*.

Storey, John. *Starting Your Own Business: No Money Down*. New York: John Wiley & Sons, Inc., 1987.

This book offers step-by-step guidance on starting a business on a shoestring. The author claims to have started his business without a rich uncle by leveraging his assets and available equity. He tells how to elicit the support of banks and venture capitalists and illustrates with experiences of some well-known entrepreneurs, like Victor Kiam of Remington and Cecil Hoge, a 75-year-old venturer who suggests moonlighting as a low-cost way to get started.

U.S. Government Books. To order the catalog, write to: Publications Order Branch, Stop: SSOP, U.S. Government Printing Office, Washington, DC 20402. Books may be charged to your Mastercard or VISA by phoning (202) 783-3238 (7:30AM–4PM).

The Business and Industry section of the U.S. Government book catalog lists 20 titles costing between $1.50 and $19.00, ppd. These and other books are also available in Government Book Stores located in Washington, DC; Birmingham, Alabama; Los Angeles and San Francisco; Denver and Pueblo, Colorado; Jacksonville, Florida; Atlanta; Chicago; Laurel, Maryland; Boston; Detroit; New York; Cleveland and Columbus, Ohio; Portland, Oregon; Philadelphia and Pittsburgh; Dallas and Houston; Seattle; and Milwaukee.

U.S. Small Business Administration. Business Development Publications. Write to the Office of Business Development, 1441 L St., NW, Washington, DC 20416.

The latest listing of 57 SBA Business Development Publications can be obtained by writing to the above address and requesting Directory 115A (3-88). Publications then can be ordered at a cost of 50¢ to $1 each by writing directly to the SBA's publications office, P.O. Box 15434, Ft. Worth, TX 76119. You can also look in the blue section of the telephone book under SBA for the number of the local SCORE office. It will usually have some of these publications available, often at no charge. For quick information, you can call the national "hot line" in Washington, DC at 1-800-368-5855 (in the DC area, call (202) 653-7561).

Venture Magazine. *Directory of Venture Capital Sources.* Venture Magazine Book Sales, 521 Fifth Ave., New York, NY 10175, 1988.

Whether for business start-ups or expansions, venture capital investors are a costly though readily available funding source. Usually these operators talk in terms of big bucks and virtually become your partner, but when you need real money and can prove your potential, this directory will lead you to the pots o' gold at the ends of dozens of rainbows.

Weitzen, H. Skip. *Infopreneurs: Turning Data into Dollars.* New York: John Wiley & Sons, Inc., 1988.

This book is right on target for our data age with seven strategies for efficiently supplying information to any kind of organization or individual. It shows how to use data banks to create new business opportunities, repackage information for new markets, speed up data access, customize data, and more.

FEDERAL AND STATE RESOURCES

GOVERNMENT OFFICES THAT CAN HELP YOU

A vast amount of information is available from governments on every level. The federal, state, county, and municipal governments often overlap and vie with each other in providing the citizen with some visible service return for his or her tax dollar. Here are five basic starting points for your governmental research:

1. The blue section in your telephone book contains all your *local* government listings. Particularly useful are the local offices of the Commerce Department, Small Business Administration, and under the latter, SCORE (Service Corps of Retired Executives).

2. Your local library contains a directory published for every field, association, bureau, trade, and kind of media.

3. Your local U.S. Congressional office is your door to Washington, DC. Congressional and Senatorial staff people will try and

dig up the information you seek. They might even have literature on hand or will get it for you.

4. State agencies in your state capital, especially the offices of business development, financial assistance, procurement assistance, and, in many cases, international trade, will have valuable information as it applies to your state.

5. Some of the bigger municipalities—San Francisco is a prime example—also have bureaus parallel to the state agencies.

Among the principal U.S. Government offices relevant to starting a small business are the following:

Department of Agriculture (DOA). This has 14 different programs designed to help landowners and producers both domestically and in international trade of their products. It covers assistance in marketing, technical development, international development, soil conservation, rural loan programs, and science and education. The general number, in addition to your local Ag office, is (202) 447-4026.

Department of Commerce (DOC). This is one of the most useful and most widely spread branches of the federal government. Each state has at least one office (see the telephone book's blue section). Under this bureau's umbrella are the following divisions:

Business Assistance Service: (202) 377-3176
Census Bureau: (202) 763-4040
Bureau of Economic Analysis: (202) 523-0777
Technical Information Service: (202) 487-4660
National Bureau of Standards: (301) 975-2762
Office of Consumer Affairs: (202) 377-5001
Minority Business: (202) 377-1936
International Trade: (202) 377-3808

and several others.

Department of Defense (DOD). While your local SBA office can give you the name and telephone number of the nearest DOD procurement representative, major military installations across the country have officers familiar with such small business liaison. The needs of this agency are so vast that it has issued its own "Defense Acquisitions Regulations" publication. The national address is: Cameron Station, Duke St., Alexandria, VA 22304-6100; phone: (202) 274-6471.

Department of Energy (DOE). This multipurpose agency manages the nation's nuclear energy program and oversees energy conservation methods and patents, and energy data collection and analysis. It has nine different sections where you can get information and help. The Washington address is: 1000 Independence Ave., SW, Washington, DC 20585; phone: (202) 586-5600.

Department of Justice (DOJ). In addition to matters of law and justice, this bureau is charged with the Immigration and Naturalization Service. If you plan to hire aliens, especially in farm and agricultural operations, check your local INS office for the latest legal caveats. There is a national toll-free line you can call: 1-800-777-7700.

Department of Labor (DOL). Here you can get information regarding employment laws and compensation, safety regulations (OSHA), discrimination, and pension plans. Eight different departments are at your service in Washington, though there is a general information number: (202) 523-6666.

Department of the Treasury (DOT). The Internal Revenue Service, Alcohol and Tobacco Information, and the manufacture of our currency come under this agency. While the IRS has offices all across the country, it has a toll-free hot line in Washington at 1-800-424-1040. The general number for all other Treasury matters is (202) 566-2041.

Environmental Protection Agency (EPA). While the EPA is a regulatory agency, it generates a lot of business geared to the control and abatement of air and water pollution; management of wastes; and control of toxic substances, radiation, and pesticides. It has a Minority Business Enterprise Construction Grants program, as well as research and procurement divisions. A free publication is available, called "Doing Business with the EPA," and a small business ombudsman will answer your questions via a national toll-free hot line: 1-800-368-5888.

Export-Import Bank (EIB). This is an independent government agency that provides financing to potential exporters, especially those who have had trouble getting loans through regular commercial channels. It has a very extensive Business Advisory Service for small businesses, which will inform you about loans, credit, procurement, and insurance. There is a national toll-free advisory hot line: 1-800-424-5201.

General Services Administration (GSA). This agency provides the federal government with property, records, construction, operation, and maintenance of buildings and communication systems, as well as property disposal, stockpiling of strategic materials, and management of the AUTOMATED DATA PROGRAM. It has 11 offices all over the country (see the following section). For $2.50 you can get a Government Printing Office publication called "Doing Business with the Federal Government." The national office is at 18th & F Sts., NW, Washington, DC 20405; phone: (202) 566-1231.

Small Business Administration (SBA). This agency in Washington has an "Answer Desk" that will refer you to the local branch you need. In 1988 more than 85,000 calls were taken, and of this number almost 85 percent asked, "How can we get the money?" The answer, of course, is that you must prepare a detailed and credible business plan before you talk to either an SBA loan officer or your local bank (which might be an SBA correspondent—that is, its loan to you will be guaranteed by the SBA, pending investigation and approval). The SBA subsidizes the Service Corps of Retired Executives, any one of whose offices—and there are 385 of them—can help you in constructing that business plan properly. If you cannot locate the SCORE office or the SBA office, call the "Answer Desk" and they'll tell you where the nearest one is located. The national toll-free hot line is 1-800-368-5855.

U.S. Customs (USC). If your business includes bringing in goods from foreign countries, that is where you get all the information on rules, costs, status, entry processes, etc. Literature may be available from: 1301 Constitution Ave., NW, Washington, DC 20229; phone: (202) 566-5286.

U.S. Post Office (USPO). If yours is a mail-order business or utilizes a lot of postal services, you ought to know about the Postal Customer Council. Meetings are held periodically between postal officials and businesspeople. Problems are worked out, and you can consult this council on the best and most economical ways to handle your mailing requirements. If you want to sell the USPO, get a free booklet from the local post office called "Let's Do Business" or call (202) 245-4818.

BUYING FROM UNCLE SAM

The world's largest "consumer" is the United States Government, but it doesn't use up everything it buys. Many small entrepreneurs have become big by taking advantage of the millions of dollars' worth of goods left over each year from the billions of dollars' worth of goods that Uncle Sam didn't need anymore. Following each of our wars, soldiers and suppliers who knew the ropes were able to target surplus Armed Services merchandise, find buyers for it, and become wealthy. The agency responsible for these sales, the U.S. General Services Administration, issues periodic lists of available merchandise, which is then sold on a bid basis by one of the ten regional GSA offices. You can get on the mailing list by contacting one of the offices listed below:

REGION I:	Comprises Connecticut, Maine, Massachussetts, New Hampshire, Rhode Island, Vermont—John McCormack Bldg., Boston, MA 02109 (617) 223-2868
REGION II:	New Jersey, New York—26 Federal Plaza, New York, NY 10278 (212) 264-1234
REGION III:	Delaware, Maryland, Pennsylvania, Virginia, West Virginia—9th and Market Sts., Philadelphia, PA 19107, (215) 597-9613
REGION IV:	Alabama, Florida, Georgia, Kentucky, Mississippi, North Carolina, South Carolina, Tennessee—1776 Peachtree St. NW, Atlanta, GA 30309, (404) 881-4661
REGION V:	Illinois, Indiana, Michigan, Minnesota, Ohio, Wisconsin—230 S. Dearborn St., Chicago, IL 60604, (312) 353-5383
REGION VI:	Iowa, Kansas, Missouri, Nebraska—1500 E. Bannister Rd., Kansas City, MO 64131, (816) 926-7203
REGION VII:	Arkansas, Louisiana, New Mexico, Oklahoma, Texas—(two locations) 819 Taylor St., Ft. Worth, TX 76102, (817) 334-3284; Federal Office Bldg., & Court House, 515 Rusk St., Houston, TX 77002, (713) 226-5787
REGION VIII:	Colorado, Montana, North Dakota, South Dakota, Utah, Wyoming—Denver Federal Center, Bldg. 41, Denver, CO 80225, (303) 234-2216
REGION IX:	Arizona, California, Hawaii, Nevada—(two locations) 525 Market St., San Francisco, CA 94105, (415) 556-2122; 300 N. Los Angeles Ave., Los Angeles, CA 90012, (212) 688-3210

REGION X: Idaho, Oregon, Washington—440 Federal Bldg., 915 Second Ave., Seattle, WA 98174, (206) 442-5556

WASHINGTON, DC: Has its own office at 7th and D Sts., SW, Washington, DC 20407, (202) 472-1804

SELLING TO UNCLE SAM

A business as big as our federal government must have a protocol—a set of rules by which potential suppliers have to abide. It is all spelled out in books and pamphlets. If you are thinking of doing business with Uncle Sam, the first thing to do is hurry to the main branch of your public library and see if the following publications are on file. If not, you can send away for them (the prices listed were in effect at the end of 1988).

"The Federal Acquisition Regulations (FAR)," U.S. Government Printing Office, Washington, DC 20402 ($143.00)

The U.S. Government Purchasing and Sales Directory, published by SBA. Order from GPO (above) ($5.50)

Selling to The Military, from GPO ($8.00)

How to Sell to U.S. Government Agencies, free from your nearest SBA office

Commerce Business Daily, published by the Department of Commerce. Order from GPO ($243 annually)

Bidders' Mailing List, available from Office of Small and Disadvantaged Business Utilization of whatever U.S. department you want to do business with. Use request form SF 129. Your local SBA office also should have these forms for the local federal procurement offices.

PASS, or Procurement Automated Source System, is a computerized listing of firms maintained by the SBA. If you register for this listing, you will have access to more than 300 government procurement centers and over 60 prime contractors. Contact your local SBA office.

Research and development funds are sometimes available and will be listed in both the Commerce Business Daily and Bidders' Mailing Lists.

BIDDING ON GOVERNMENT CONTRACTS

To bid on government contracts, write to or call the appropriate, alphabetically listed departments or agencies.

Agriculture

U.S. Department of Agriculture, Agricultural Marketing Service, Procurement and Contracting Section, Property and Procurement Branch, 14th St. & Independence Ave., SW, 0758 South Bldg. Washington, DC 20250, (202) 447-3457

Armed Services

Defense Logistic Agency, Small Business and Economic Utilization Adviser, Cameron Station, Rm. 4B110, Alexandria, VA 22314, (202) 274-6471

Army and Air Force Exchange Service, 3911 S. Walton Walker, Dallas, TX 75222, (214) 330-2225.

Army Corps of Engineers, U.S. Army Engineering Division HQ, Pentagon, Washington, DC 20310, (202) 693-0201

Naval Aviation Supply Office, 700 Robbins Ave., Rm. 201, Bldg. One, Philadelphia, PA 19111, (215) 697-2806

Veterans Administration, Marketing Division, VA Marketing Center, P.O. Box 76, Hines, IL 60141, (312) 681-6782

Environmental Protection Agency

Procurement and Contracts Management Division, Minority Business/Small Business Section, 401 M St., NW, Washington, DC 20460, (202) 755-0616

Food and Drug Administration

Procurement, Property and Facilities Management Branch, 5600 Fishers Lane, Rm. 5020, Rockville, MD 20857, (301) 433-3250

Federal Trade Commission

Procurement and Contracting Branch, 633 Indiana Ave., NW, Washington, DC 20580, (202) 723-1133

General Accounting Office

Procurement Branch, 441 G St., NW, Rm. 3130, Washington, DC 20460, (202) 275-3455

General Services Administration

Business Service Center, 18th & F Sts., NW, Washington, DC 20405, (202) 566-1231

Also has offices in Boston, New York, Philadelphia, Atlanta, Chicago, Kansas City, Fort Worth, Denver, San Francisco, Los Angeles, and Seattle.

Government Printing Office

Printing Procurement Department, N. Capital & H Sts., NW, Rm. C-883, Washington, DC 20401, (202) 275-2265

Health and Human Services

U.S. Department of Office of Grants and Procurement, Office of the Assistant Secretary for Management and Budget, H.H. Humphrey Bldg., 200 Independence Ave., SW, Rm. 513-D, Washington, DC 20201, (202) 655-4000

Housing & Urban Development

U.S. Department of Office Procurement and Contracts, Procurement and Grants Division, 451 Seventh St., NW, 9th Fl., Washington, DC 20410, (202) 724-0036

Internal Revenue Service

Contracts M Procurement Section, 11th & Constitution Ave., NW, Rm. 1237, Washington, DC 20224, (202) 566-3656

Labor Department

Division of Procurement, Office of Administrative Services, 200 Constitution Ave., NW, Rm. 51514, Washington, DC 20210, (202) 523-6451

National Institutes of Health

Procurement Branch, Division of Administration Services, 9000 Rockville Pike, Bldg. 31, Rm. 3C39, Bethesda, MD 20014, (301) 496-3181

Postal Service

Procurement and Supply Program, Plans and Management Division, 474 L'Enfant Plaza West, SW, Washington, DC 20260, (202) 245-5663

Small Business Administration

Procurement and Grants Management, 1441 L St., NW, Rm. 221, Washington, DC 20416, (202) 653-6639

STATE AGENCIES THAT HELP SMALL BUSINESS PEOPLE

States are actively helping entrepreneurs in five areas of business: business development, financial assistance, procurement assistance, minority/women opportunities, and international trade. The following is a state-by-state list of Development Offices you can contact for information and assistance. Virtually all of them have complimentary publications available, especially in the areas of business development and international trade. Inquire about any such publications when you make your initial contact.

ALABAMA: Development Office, State Capitol, Montgomery, AL 36130, 1-800-248-0033 or (205) 263-0048

ALASKA: Division of Business Development, P.O. Box D, Juneau, AK 99811, (907) 465-2017

ARIZONA: Department of Commerce, 1700 W. Washington St., 4th Fl., Phoenix, AZ 85007, (602) 255-5705

ARKANSAS: Small Business Information Center, One State Capitol Mall, Rm.4C300, Little Rock, AR 77201, (501) 682-3358

CALIFORNIA: Office of Small Business, 1121 L St., Suite 600, Sacramento, CA 95814, (916) 445-6545

COLORADO: Business Information Center, 1525 Sherman St., Rm. 110, Denver, CO 80203, (303) 866-3933

CONNECTICUT: Small Business Services, 210 Washington St., Hartford, CT 06106, (203) 566-4051

DELAWARE:	Development Office, 99 King's Highway, P.O. Box 1401, Dover, DE 19903, (302) 736-4271
DISTRICT OF COLUMBIA:	Office of Business and Economic Development, 7th Fl., 1111 E St., NW, Washington, DC 20004, (202) 727-6600
FLORIDA:	Bureau of Business Assistance, 107 Gaines St., Tallahassee, FL 32339-2000, 1-800-342-0771 or (904) 488-9357
GEORGIA:	Department of Industry and Trade, 230 Peachtree Rd. NW, Atlanta, GA 30303, (404) 656-3584
HAWAII:	Small Business Information Service, 250 S. King St., Rm. 727, Honolulu, HI 96813, (808) 548-7645
IDAHO:	Economic Development Division, Department of Commerce, State Capitol, Rm. 108, Boise, ID 83720, (208) 334-3416
ILLINOIS:	Small Business Assistance Bureau, 620 E. Adams St., Springfield, IL 62701, 1-800-252-2923 or (217) 785-6282
INDIANA:	Division of Business Expansion, Department of Commerce, One North Capital, Suite 700, Indianapolis, IN 46204-2288, 1-800-824-2476 or (317) 232-3527
IOWA:	Bureau of Small Business Development, 200 E. Grand Ave., Des Moines, IA 50309, 1-800-532-1216 or (515) 281-8310
KANSAS:	Division of Existing Industry Development, 400 S.W. Eighth St., 5th Fl., Topeka, KS 66603, (913) 296-5298

KENTUCKY: Small Business Division, Capitol Plaza, 22nd Fl., Frankfort, KY 40601, 1-800-626-2250 or (502) 564-4252

LOUISIANA: Development Division, Office of Commerce and Industry, P.O. Box 94185, Baton Rouge, LA 70804-9185, (504) 342-5365

MAINE: Business Development Division, State Development Office, State House, Augusta, ME 04333, 1-800-872-3838 or (207) 289-2659

MARYLAND: Office of Business and Industrial Development, 45 Calvert St., Annapolis, MD 21401, 1-800-654-7336 or (301) 974-2946

MASSACHUSETTS: Small Business Assistance Division, 100 Cambridge St., 13th Fl., Boston, MA 02202, (617) 727-4005

MICHIGAN: Business Ombudsman, Department of Commerce, P.O. Box 30107, Lansing, MI 48909, 1-800-232-2727 or (517) 373-6241

MINNESOTA: Small Business Assistance Office, 900 American Center, 150 E. Kellogg Blvd., St. Paul, MN 55101, 1-800-652-9747 or (612) 296-3871

MISSISSIPPI: Small Business Bureau, 3825 Ridgewood Rd., Jackson, MS 39211-6453, (601) 982-6231

MISSOURI: Small Business Development Office, P.O. Box 118, Jefferson City, MO 65102, (314) 751-4981/8411

MONTANA: Business Assistance Center, 1424 Ninth Ave., Helena, MT 59620, 1-800-221-8015 or (406) 444-3923

NEBRASKA:	Small Business Division, P.O. Box 94666, 301 Centennial Mall S., Lincoln, NE 68509, (402) 471-4167
NEVADA:	Office of Community Service, 1100 East William, Suite 116, Carson City, NV 89710, (702) 885-4602
NEW HAMPSHIRE:	Office of Industrial Development, 105 Loudon Rd., Prescott Park, Bldg. 2, Concord, NH 03301, (603) 271-2591
NEW JERSEY:	Office of Small Business Assistance, 1 W. State St. (CN-835), Trenton, NJ 08625, (609) 984-4442
NEW MEXICO:	Economic Development Division, 1100 St. Francis Dr., Santa Fe, NM 87503, 1-800-545-2040 or (505) 827-0300
NEW YORK:	Division for Small Business, 230 Park Ave., Rm. 834, New York, NY 10169, (212) 309-0400
NORTH CAROLINA:	Small Business Development Division, Dobbs Bldg., Rm. 2019, 430 N. Salisbury St., Raleigh, NC 27611, (919) 733-7980
NORTH DAKOTA:	Small Business Coordinator, Economic Development Commission, Liberty Memorial Bldg., Bismarck, ND 58505, 1-800-472-2100 or (701) 224-2810
OHIO:	Small and Developing Business Division, P.O. Box 1001, Columbus, OH 43266-0101, 1-800-282-1085 or (614) 466-1876
OKLAHOMA:	Oklahoma Department of Commerce, 6601 Broadway Ext., Oklahoma, OK 73116, (405) 521-2401

OREGON:	Economic Development Department, 595 Cottage St. NE, Salem, OR 97310, 1-800-233-3306 or 547-7842; or (503) 373-1200
PENNSYLVANIA:	Small Business Action Center, Department of Commerce, 404 Forum Bldg., Harrisburg, PA 17120, (717) 783-5700
PUERTO RICO:	Commonwealth, Department of Commerce, Box S, 4275 Old San Juan Station, San Juan, PR 00905, (809) 758-4747
RHODE ISLAND:	Small Business Development Division, 7 Jackson Walkway, Providence, RI 02903, (401) 277-2601
SOUTH CAROLINA:	Business Development M Assistance Division, P.O. Box 927, Columbia, SC 29202, 1-800-922-6684 or (803) 737-0400
SOUTH DAKOTA:	Governor's Office of Economic Development, Capital Lake Plaza, Pierre, SD 57501, 1-800-952-3625 or (605) 773-5032
TENNESSEE:	Small Business Office, 320 Sixth Ave. N., 7th Fl., Rachel Jackson Bldg., Nashville, TN 37219, 1-800-922-6684 or (803) 737-0400
TEXAS:	Small Business Division, P.O. Box 12728 Capitol Station, 410 E. Fifth St., Austin, TX 78711, (512) 472-5059
UTAH:	Small Business Development Center, 660 S. Second St., Rm. 418, Salt Lake City, UT 84111, (801) 581-7905
VERMONT:	Agency of Development and Community Affairs, The Pavillion, Montpelier, VT 05602, 1-800-622-4553 or (802) 828-3221

VIRGINIA: Small Business and Financial Services, 1000 Washington Bldg., Richmond, VA 23219, (804) 786-3791

WASHINGTON: Small Business Development Center, 441 Todd Hall, Washington State University, Pullman, WA 99164, (509) 335-1576

WEST VIRGINIA: Small Business Development Center Division, Governor's Office, Capital Complex, Charleston, WVA 25305, (304) 348-2960

WISCONSIN: Small Business Ombudsman, Department of Development, 123 W. Washington Ave., P.O. Box 7970, Madison, WI 53707, 1-800-435-7287 or (608) 266-0562

WYOMING: Economic Development and Stabilization Board, Herschler Bldg., 3rd Fl. E., Cheyenne, WY 82002, (307) 777-7287

PRIVATE-SECTOR RESOURCES

FIFTY STATE CHAMBERS OF COMMERCE

Chambers of Commerce can be found in over 4500 communities in the United States. In most cases these chambers are full-time offices that serve as rallying points for the town's or city's business-people. They provide information and statistics on local economic conditions and access to local leaders and decision makers. More-over, chambers, being established, can lend new entrepreneurs an aura of prestige and offer an opportunity for networking with other members. A membership decal on your business door can be useful, both psychologically and practically. In addition to the local offices, every state has a state chamber. To get information about your state chamber's programs, or referral to your nearest hometown chamber, consult the following list:

ALABAMA: Business Council of Alabama, 468 South
                          Perry St., P.O. Box 76, Montgomery, AL
                          36195, (205) 834-6000

ALASKA: Alaska State Chamber of Commerce, 310 Second St., Juneau, AK 99801, (907) 586-2323

ARIZONA: Arizona Chamber of Commerce, 1366 E. Thomas Rd., Suite 202, Phoenix, AZ 85012, (602) 248-9172

ARKANSAS: Arkansas State Chamber of Commerce, P.O. Box 3645, 100 Main St., Suite 510, Little Rock, AR 72203-3645, (501) 374-9225

CALIFORNIA: California Chamber of Commerce, 1027 10th St., P.O. Box 1736, Sacramento, CA 95808, (916) 444-6670

COLORADO: Colorado Association of Commerce & Industry, 1860 Lincoln St., Suite 550, Denver, CO 80295-0501, (303) 831-7411

CONNECTICUT: Connecticut Business & Industry Association, Inc., 370 Asylum St., Hartford, CT 06103, (203) 547-1661

DELAWARE: Delaware State Chamber of Commerce, Inc., One Commerce Center, Suite 200, Wilmington, DE 19801, (302) 655-7221

FLORIDA: Florida Chamber of Commerce, 136 S. Bronought St., P.O. Box 11309, Tallahassee, FL 32302, (904) 222-2831

GEORGIA: Business Council of Georgia, 1280 S. CNN Center, Atlanta, GA 30303-2705, (404) 223-2264

HAWAII: The Chamber of Commerce of Hawaii, Dillingham Bldg., 735 Bishop St., Honolulu, HI 96813, (808) 531-4111

IDAHO: Idaho Association of Commerce & Industry, 805 Idaho St., P.O. Box 389, Suite 200, Boise, ID 83701, (208) 243-1849

ILLINOIS: Illinois State Chamber of Commerce, 20 N. Wacker Dr., Chicago, IL 60606, (312) 372-7373

INDIANA: Indiana State Chamber of Commerce, Inc., Indiana Commerce Center, One N. Capitol, Suite 200, Indianapolis, IN 46204-2248, (317) 634-6407

IOWA: Iowa Association of Business & Industry, 706 Employers Mutual Bldg., 717 Mulberry St., Des Moines, IA 50309, 1-800-532-1406 (Toll Free—Iowa Only), (515) 244-6149

KANSAS: Kansas Chamber of Commerce & Industry, 500 Bank IV Tower, One Townsite Plaza, Topeka, KS 66603, (913) 357-6321

KENTUCKY: Kentucky Chamber of Commerce, Versailles Rd., P.O. Box 817, Frankfort, KY 40602, (502) 695-4700

LOUISIANA: Louisiana Association of Business & Industry, P.O. Box 80258, Baton Rouge, LA 70898-0258, (504) 928-5388

MAINE: Maine Chamber of Commerce & Industry, 126 Sewall St., Augusta, ME 04330, (207) 623-4568

MARYLAND: Maryland Chamber of Commerce, 60 West St., Suite 405, Annapolis, MD 21401, (301) 269-0642

MASSACHUSETTS: Massachusetts Association of Chamber of Commerce Executives, % Wellesley Chamber of Commerce, 287 Linden St., P.O. Box 715, Wellesley, MA 02181, (617) 235-2446

MICHIGAN: Michigan State Chamber of Commerce, 600 S. Walnut St., Lansing, MI 48933, (517) 371-2100

MINNESOTA: Minnesota Chamber of Commerce & Industry, 300 Hanover Bldg., 480 Cedar St., St. Paul, MN 55101, (612) 292-4650

MISSISSIPPI: Mississippi Economic Council, 656 N. State St., P.O. Box 1849, Jackson, MS 39215-1849, (601) 969-0022

MISSOURI: Missouri Chamber of Commerce, P.O. Box 149, Jefferson City, MO 65102, (314) 634-3511

MONTANA: Montana Chamber of Commerce, 110 Neill Ave., P.O. Box 1730, Helena, MT 59624, (406) 442-2405

NEBRASKA: Nebraska Association of Commerce & Industry, 1320 Lincoln Mall, P.O. Box 95128, Lincoln, NE 68509, (402) 474-4422

NEVADA: Nevada Chamber of Commerce Association, P.O. Box 3499, Reno, NV 89505, (702) 786-3030

NEW ENGLAND: New England Council, Inc., 120 Boylston St., 8th Fl., Boston, MA 02116, (617) 542-2580

NEW HAMPSHIRE: Business and Industry Association of New Hampshire, 23 School St., Concord, NH 03301, (603) 224-5388

NEW JERSEY: New Jersey State Chamber of Commerce, 5 Commerce St., Newark, NJ 07102, (201) 623-7070

NEW MEXICO: Association of Commerce & Industry of New Mexico, 4001 Indian School Rd.,

	N.E., Suite 333, Albuquerque, NM 87110, (505) 265-5847
NEW YORK:	Business Council of New York State, 152 Washington Ave., Albany, NY 12210, (518) 465-7511
NORTH CAROLINA:	North Carolina Citizens for Business and Industry, 336 Fayetteville St. Mall, P.O. Box 2508, Raleigh, NC 27602, (919) 828-0758
NORTH DAKOTA:	Greater North Dakota Association/State Chamber of Commerce, P.O. Box 2467, Fargo, ND 58108, (701) 237-9461
OHIO:	Ohio Chamber of Commerce, 35 E. Gay St., 2nd Fl., Columbus, OH 43215-3181, (614) 228-4201
OKLAHOMA:	Oklahoma Chamber of Commerce & Industry, 4020 N. Lincoln Blvd., Oklahoma City, OK 73105, (405) 424-4003
OREGON:	Associated Oregon Industries, Inc., 1149 Court St., N.E., P.O. Box 12519, Salem, OR 97309, (503) 588-0050
PENNSYLVANIA:	Pennsylvania Chamber of Business & Industry, 222 N. Third St., Harrisburg, PA 17101, (717) 255-3252
PUERTO RICO:	Chamber of Commerce of Puerto Rico, 100 Tetuan St., Old San Juan, PR 00904, (809) 721-6060
RHODE ISLAND:	Rhode Island Chamber of Commerce Federation, 91 Park St., Providence, RI 02908, (401) 272-1400
SOUTH CAROLINA:	South Carolina Chamber of Commerce, Bankers Trust Tower, 1301 Gervais St.,

Suite 520, P.O. Box 11278, Columbia, SC 29211, (803) 799-4601

SOUTH DAKOTA: Industry and Commerce Association of South Dakota, P.O. Box 190, Pierre, SD 57501, (605) 224-6161

TENNESSEE: Tennessee Manufacturers and Taxpayers Association, 226 Capitol Blvd., Suite 800, Nashville, TN 37219, (615) 256-5141

TEXAS: Texas State Chamber of Commerce*, 206 W. 13th, Suite A, Austin, TX 78701, (512) 472-1594
* A federation of four regional chambers of commerce in Texas

East Texas Chamber of Commerce, P.O. Box 1592, Longview, TX 75606, (214) 757-4444

Rio Grande Valley Chamber of Commerce, P.O. Box 1499, Weslaco, TX 78596, (512) 968-3141

South Texas Chamber of Commerce, 6222 N.W. Interstate 10, Suite 100, San Antonio, TX 78201, (512) 732-8185

West Texas Chamber of Commerce, 155 Hickory St., P.O. Box 1561, Abilene, TX 79604, (915) 677-4325

VERMONT: Vermont State Chamber of Commerce, P.O. Box 37, Montpelier, VT 05602, (802) 223-3443, (802) 229-0154

VIRGINIA: The Virginia Chamber of Commerce, 9 S. Fifth St., Richmond, VA 23219, (804) 644-1607

WASHINGTON:	Association of Washington Business, P.O. Box 658, Olympia, WA 98507, (206) 943-1600
WEST VIRGINIA:	West Virginia Chamber of Commerce, 1101 Kanawha Valley Bldg., P.O. Box 2789, Charleston, WV 25330, (304) 342-1115
WISCONSIN:	Wisconsin Association of Manufacturers & Commerce, 501 E. Washington Ave., P.O. Box 352, Madison, WI 53701, (608) 258-3400

NATIONAL BUSINESS ORGANIZATIONS

In addition to the chambers of commerce, a number of other business organizations exist that you will want to know about, and perhaps investigate for membership. Below are some of the most prominent general ones and several more geared to special interests.

General

American Entrepreneurs Association. This privately promoted and managed organization is built around *Entrepreneur Magazine* and more than 250 detailed "how to" manuals on specific small businesses. Address: 2392 Morris Ave., Irvine, CA 92714; phone: (714) 261-2325.

National Association for the Cottage Industry. A membership organization that monitors national and state regulations, provides general information, gives discounts on services, conducts seminars, publishes "Cottage Connection" newsletter. Address: P.O. Box 14850, Chicago, IL, 60614.

National Association of Development Companies. A union of certified development companies that participate in SBA lending programs (Section 503 companies), providing small entrepreneurs with long-term fixed-asset financing. Address: 1730 Rhode Island Ave., NW, Suite 209, Washington, DC 20036; phone: (202) 785-8484.

National Association of Entrepreneurs. NAE is essentially a private networking organization for small business operators, allowing them to exchange ideas, information, and support. Has chartered chapters in cities of 25,000 or more population. Offers workshops, books, tapes, annual conference. Address: 2378 S. Broadway, Denver, CO 80210; phone: (303) 426-1166.

National Association of Manufacturers. NAM is a national 13,500-member association, two-thirds of which are manufacturers with fewer than 500 employees. However, the association's members account for 80 percent of America's industrial capacity. Has 100 subject specialists to help members with problems and to influence legislation. Address: 1331 Pennsylvania Ave., Suite 1500, Washington, DC 20004-1703; phone: (202) 637-3000.

National Association of Small Business Investment Companies. This is a group of over 400 small business investment companies (SBICs) that are privately capitalized and owned, and licensed by the SBA. Provides long-term financing, equity capital, and management assistance. Based heavily on job creation. Address: 1156 15th St., NW, Suite 1101, Washington, DC 20005; phone: (202) 833-8230.

The National Federation of Independent Business. NFIB boasts a membership of more than 500,000 small and independent businesses. Conducts surveys and studies, lobbies, produces educational material, holds conferences. Address: 600 Maryland Ave., SW, Suite 700, Washington, DC 20024; phone: (202) 554-9000.

National Small Business United. This is an umbrella group representing semi-independent business organizations in Ohio, Wisconsin, New England, Pennsylvania Triangle, Michigan, Texas, Denver area, Illinois, Kentucky, Georgia, and California. Founded 1937. Provides regional networking information, newsletters, legislative liaison. Address: 1155 15th St.,NW, Suite 710, Washington, DC 20005; phone: (202) 293-8830.

Specialized

Center for Neighborhood Technology. Makes available technical assistance and publications to neighborhood economic development organizations. Works in housing, energy, agriculture (urban), solar installations, waste recycling. Has newsletter and other publications. Address: 2125 W. North Ave., Chicago, IL 60647.

Community Economic Development Clearinghouse. For alternative community, individual, and organizational enterprises. Offers information, referrals, networking. Publishes computerized "Catalog of Ideas" and a newsletter, and has video presentation. Address: 628 Clark Hall, University of Missouri, Columbia, MO 65211.

The Crafts Center. This is a national association of artisans and craftspeople, suppliers and government organizations. Maintains good data base, publishes "Crafts News" and an international directory. Address: 2001 O St.,NW, Washington, DC 20005.

Inventors Workshop International Educational Foundation. Educational foundation for inventors. Offers guidance on development, protection, market testing, etc. Provides opportunity for networking through local chapters. Send SASE for info and copies of their publications. P.O. Box 251, Tarzana, CA 91356; phone: (818) 344-3375.

National Association of Home-Based Businesses. About 1000 members. Provides networking opportunities, joint marketing services, association newspaper. Address: P.O. Box 30220, Baltimore, MD 21270.

National Cooperative Business Association. Trade association for coops. Offers legislative assistance, training programs, newspaper. Address: 1401 New York Ave., NW, Suite 1100, Washington, DC 20005.

Small Business Foundation of America. Not a membership organization, but a research outfit that helps small business groups to organize, Publishes newsletters and books. Address: 20 Park Plaza, Boston, MA 02116.

Small Business Service Bureau. A private, national association with 35,000 members. It focuses on management assistance, legislative advocacy, insurance benefits, consultation on trading with the People's Republic of China. Address: P.O. Box 1441, Worcester, MA 01601.

Women and Minority

National Association of Black and Minority Chambers of Commerce. Funded by the U.S. Department of Commerce in 1979, primarily in the tourist and convention field, it networks through 350 chambers of commerce. Address: 654 13th St., Oakland, CA 94612-1241; phone: (415) 451-9231.

National Association of Investment Companies. NAIC is a trade association representing companies that invest in small businesses owned by socially or economically disadvantaged entrepreneurs. Address: 915 15th St., NW, Suite 700, Washington, DC 20005; phone: (202) 347-8600.

National Association of Minority Contractors. Founded in 1969 to support the needs of minority contractors. Offers newsletter, films, education, seminars, networking. Address: 806 15th St., NW, Suite 340, Washington, DC 20005; phone: (202) 347-8259.

National Association of Women Business Owners. Has about 3000 members in 37 local chapters nationwide. Offers monthly local programs, national annual conference. Address: 600 S. Federal St., Suite 400, Chicago, IL 60605; phone: (312) 922-0465.

National Business League. This is the voice of black business on Capitol Hill. It has 127 local chapters covering a variety of industries.

Established in 1900. Address: 4324 Georgia Ave. NW, Washington, DC 20011; phone: (202) 829-5900.

U.S. Hispanic Chamber of Commerce. Represents interests of over 400,000 Hispanic-owned enterprises. Develops opportunities with major corporations and governments. Has over 200 chambers. Address: 4900 Main Street, Suite 700, Kansas City, MO 64112; phone: (816) 531-6363.

SELECTED NATIONAL PROFESSIONAL AND TRADE ASSOCIATIONS

Of considerable potential value are trade associations in your special field. Among the thousands that exist, we have selected 48 of the major ones, representing a cross section of commerce and industry. Each one holds meetings, often in local chapters or councils, where opportunities exist to learn about your business, and publishes newsletters and trade journals that can be of inestimable value in the continuing education and success of the entrepreneur.

American Bankers Association, 1120 Connecticut Ave., NW, Washington, DC 20036, (202) 663-5000.

American Farm Bureau Federation, 225 W. Touhy Ave., Park Ridge, IL 60068, (312) 399-5700.

American Council of Life Insurance, 1001 Pennsylvania Ave., NW, Ste. 500, Washington, DC 20004-2599, (202) 624-2000.

American Electronics Association, 5201 Great America Parkway, Santa Clara, CA 95054, (408) 987-4200.

American Financial Services Association, 1101 14th St., NW, 4th Floor, Washington, DC 20005, (202) 289-0400.

American Health Care Association, 1200 15th St., NW, 8th Floor, Washington, DC 20005, (202) 833-2050.

American Hotel and Motel Association, 888 Seventh Ave., New York, NY 10106, (212) 265-4506.

American Institute of Certified Public Accountants, 1211 Avenue of the Americas, New York, NY 10036, (212) 575-6200.

American Insurance Association, 85 John St., New York, NY 10038, (212) 669-0400.

American Petroleum Institute, 1220 L St., NW, Washington, DC 20005, (202) 682-8000.

American Retail Federation, 1616 H St., NW, Ste. 600, Washington, DC 20006, (202) 783-7971.

American Society of Association Executives, 1575 Eye St., NW, Washington, DC 20005, (202) 626-2723.

American Society of Travel Agents, 1101 King St., Alexandria, VA 22314, (703) 739-2782.

American Trucking Association, 2200 Mill Rd., Alexandria, VA 22314, (703) 838-1800.

Association of American Publishers, 220 E. 23rd Street, New York, NY 10016, (212) 689-8920.

Associated Builders and Contractors, Inc., 729 15th St., NW, Washington, DC 20005, (202) 637-8800.

Associated General Contractors of America, 1957 E St., NW, Washington, DC 20006, (202) 393-2040.

Automotive Parts and Accessories Association, 5100 Forbes Blvd., Lanham, MD 20706, (301) 459-9110.

Automotive Service Association, P.O. Box 929, Bedford, TX 76021, (817) 283-6205.

Automotive Service Industry Association, 444 N. Michigan Ave., Chicago, IL 60611, (312) 836-1300.

Computer & Business Equipment Manufacturers Association, 311 First St., NW, Suite 500, Washington, DC 20001, (202) 737-8888.

Computer Software and Services Information Industry, 1300 N. 17th St., Suite 300, Arlington, VA 22209, (703) 522-5055.

Electronic Industries Association, 2001 Eye St., NW, Washington, DC 20006, (202) 457-4900.

Food Marketing Institute, 1750 K St., NW, Suite 700, Washington, DC 20006, (202) 452-8444.

Grocery Manufacturers Association, 1010 Wisconsin Ave., NW, Suite 800, Washington, DC 20007, (202) 337-9400.

Health Industry Distributors Association, 1701 Pennsylvania Ave., NW, Suite 470, Washington, DC 20006, (202) 659-0050.

Health Industry Manufacturers Association, 1030 15th St., NW, Suite 1100, Washington, DC 20005, (202) 452-8240.

Independent Insurance Agents of America, Inc., 100 Church St., Suite 1901, New York, NY 10007, (212) 285-2500.

Independent Petroleum Association of America, 1101 16th St., NW, 2nd Floor, Washington, DC 20036, (202) 857-4722.

Information Industry Association, 555 New Jersey Ave., NW, Suite 800, Washington, DC 20001, (202) 639-8262.

International Association for Financial Planning, Two Concourse Parkway, Suite 800, Atlanta, GA 30328, (404) 395-1605.

International Communications Industries Association, 3150 Spring St., Fairfax, VA 22031-2399, (703) 273-7200.

National Association of Broadcasters, 1771 N St., NW, Washington, DC 20036, (202) 429-5300.

National Association of Chain Drug Stores, P.O. Box 14177-49 Alexandria, VA 22314, (703) 549-3001.

National Association of Convenience Stores, 1605 King St., Alexandria, VA 22314-2792, (703) 684-3600.

National Association of Home Builders, 15th and M Sts., NW, Washington, DC 20005, (202) 822-0200.

National Association of Realtors, 403 N. Michigan Ave., Chicago, IL 60611, (312) 329-8200.

National Association of Truck Stop Operators, P.O. Box 1285, Alexandria, VA 22313-1285, (703) 549-2100.

National Association of Wholesaler-Distributors, 1725 K St., NW, Suite 710, Washington, DC 20006, (202) 872-0885.

National Automobile Dealers Association, 8400 Westpark Dr., McLean, VA 22102, (703) 821-7000.

National Business Incubators Association, 114 N. Hanover St., Carlisle, PA 17013, (717) 249-4508.

National Forest Products Association, 1250 Connecticut Ave., NW, Suite 200, Washington, DC 20036, (202) 463-2700.

National Home Furnishing Association, 220 W. Gerry Drive, Wood Dale, IL 60191, (312) 595-0200.

National Industrial Transportation League, 1090 Vermont Ave., NW, Suite 410, Washington, DC 20005, (202) 842-3870.

National Lumber & Building Materials Dealers Association, 40 Ivy St., SE, Washington, DC 20003, (202) 547-2230.

National Restaurant Association, 311 First St., NW, Washington, DC 20001, (202) 638-6100.

Printing Industries of America, Inc., 1730 N. Lynn St., Arlington, VA 22209, (703) 841-8100.

Travel Industry Association of America, 1133 21st St., NW, Washington, DC 20036, (202) 293-1433.

TEN INSTRUCTIONAL OFFERINGS FOR YOUTH ENTREPRENEURS

There always have been youngsters who start at age 10 or so to earn money—whether delivering newspapers, selling Girl Scout Cookies, or peddling nostrums—working toward a bike, or a future education. These days more and more high school and collegiate entrepreneur programs are being established to accommodate young businesspeople. High schools also have business-oriented organizations, such as Junior Achievement and Future Farmers of America, that conduct programs aimed at promoting independent enterprise. The Small Business Administration, through its many field offices, has placed special emphasis on a Youth Entrepreneurs program. The SBA's subsidized counseling organization, SCORE, *also* will help young entrepreneurs as well as older ones with information and special training in its 385 locations. Here are a few more resources in audiovisual and print media:

1. The National Federation of Independent Business offers a film series entitled "I Can Do It!"—three approximately one-hour

films accompanied by a teacher's guide. Available either in 16mm or ½" VHS and Beta cassettes. Write to NFIB at 150 W. 20th Ave., San Mateo, CA 94403 or 600 Maryland Ave., SW, Suite 700, Washington, DC 20024.

2. "Pack Your Own Chute" is a 30-minute motivational film on personal responsibility. Available in 16mm format from Ramic Productions, 3505 Cadillac Ave., Costa Mesa, CA 92626-1435.

3. Walt Disney Educational Media has produced a series of four films under the general title, "Fergi Builds a Business." The films follow a group of youths as they start and develop a T-shirt business. Each is in film-strip format with cassette, 18 to 25 minutes each, with a 20-page teacher's guide. Address: 500 Buena Vista St., Burbank, CA 91521.

4. "Open for Business" is a field-tested series of six 30-minute videocassettes, accompanied by a teaching guide, on the six basic phases of starting and operating a business. This is primarily for school or corporate use, as the cost is $790 for the set. Available from: Maryland Instructional Television, 11767 Bonita Ave., Owings Mills, MD 21117.

5. The Association of Collegiate Entrepreneurs publishes a newspaper, "ACE Action," that is good for networking and information sharing. Write to: ACE, Wichita State University, 1845 N. Fairmount, Wichita, KS 67208.

6. A three-level instructional program with 18 instructional units featuring a progressive "going into business" project is available from The National Center for Research in Vocational Education (PACE), Ohio State University, 1960 Kenny Rd., Columbus, OH 43210-1090.

7. *Entrepreneurship Education* is a three-volume set of printed lesson materials divided into nineteen 50-minute sessions. Available from Curriculum Publication Clearinghouse, 76B Horrabin Hall, Western Illinois University, Macomb, IL 61455.

8. The U.S. Government Printing Office (Washington, DC 20402, Att: Superintendent of Documents) has produced an outstanding four-volume set entitled *Small Business Management*. The first three books are a course in entrepreneurship and small-business management, while the fourth volume is composed of miniproblems for use with the previous teaching material. It is aimed principally at business students.

9. *Entrepreneurship Training Components (ETC)* is a set of three guide books plus a student's and a teacher's manual, aimed at the vocational-high school level. Offered by the Wisconsin Vocational Studies Center, University of Wisconsin, 1025 W. Johnson St., Madison, WI 53706.

10. *Achieving Success in Small Business*, from the same Wisconsin source, consists of 12 home-study modules and an equal number of accompanying audio cassettes, plus a study guide. This program is best utilized with a trained counselor or teacher.

CENTERS FOR HIGH-TECH ASSISTANCE

For anyone whose business venture includes the manufacture, research, sale, or servicing of high-technology products, there are some valuable sources of assistance. Of the two most generalized resources, first is the U.S. Government-operated bureau that is now called the National Institute of Standards and Technology (formerly the Bureau of Standards). The Institute has a model workshop where the latest high-tech innovations, such as robots, are tested. Information on innovations and procedures are passed on to private individuals and companies in order to make them more efficient and competitive in the international marketplace. Address: Room A-617, Gaithersburg, MD 20899; phone: (301) 975-4009.

There is also the Manufacturing Productivity Center operated by the IIT Research Institute (10 W. 35th St., Chicago, IL 60616; phone: (312) 567-4800). This center provides information on new manufacturing techniques and acts as a liaison between other technological companies. It is, in turn, the source of the following

33 manufacturing technology centers located in 16 states—a partial list—that you might want to consult if you are interested in this area of manufacturing.

The CADD/CAM Institute, 408 Cedar Bluss Road, Suite 383, Knoxville, TN 37923, 1-800-CADD/CAM or (615) 693-3378.

Center for Automated Design & Manufacturing, College of Engineering, Oklahoma State University, 111 Engineering North, Stillwater, OK 74078, (405) 624-6055.

Center for Automation Research, University of Maryland, College Park, MD 20742-3411, (301) 454-4526

Center for Manufacturing Engineering, The Technological Institute, Northwestern University, 2145 Sheridan Road, Evanston, IL 60208, (312) 491-5066.

Center for Manufacturing Productivity and Technology Transfer, Rensselaer Polytechnic Institute, Room 9015, CII, Troy, NY 12180, (518) 276-6021.

Center for Manufacturing Technology (CMT), 10200 Anderson Way, Cincinnati, OH 45242, (513) 984-7272.

Center for Metals Fabrication, 505 King Avenue, Columbus, OH 43201-2693, (614) 424-5828.

Center for Near Net Shape Manufacturing, College of Engineering, Drexel University, Philadelphia, PA 19104, (215) 895-1541, (215) 895-2322.

Center for Robotics and Integrated Manufacturing, College of Engineering, University of Michigan, Ann Arbor, MI 48109, (313) 764-6565.

Center for Welding Research, The Ohio State University, 190 West 19th Avenue, Columbus, OH 43210, (614) 292-6814.

Computer Integrated Manufacturing Systems Program (CIMS), College of Engineering, Georgia Institute of Technology, Atlanta, GA 30332-0406, (404) 894-4133.

Manufacturing Technology Information Analysis Center (MTIAC), Cresap, A Towers Perrin Co., 200 West Madison Street, Chicago, IL 60606, (312) 567-4730.

Center for Advance Manufacturing, College of Engineering, Clemson University, Clemson, SC 29634-0921, (803) 656-3291.

Flexible Manufacturing Laboratory, The Ohio State University, 1971 Neil Avenue, Room 210, Columbus, OH 43210-1271, (614) 292-2980.

Georgia Productivity Center, Georgia Technology Research Institute, 219 O'Keefe Building, Atlanta, GA 30332, (404) 894-6101.

Industrial Extension Service, North Carolina State University, School of Engineering, Box 7902, Raleigh, NC 27695-7902, (919) 737-3262.

Industrial Technology Institute, P.O. Box 1485, Ann Arbor, MI 48106, (313) 769-4000.

Institute of Advanced Manufacturing Sciences, Inc. (IAMS), 1111 Edison Drive, Cincinnati, OH 45216-2265, (513) 948-2100.

Institute for Metal Forming, Whitaker Lab. #5, Bethlehem, PA 18015, (215) 758-4233.

International Flexible Automation Center (INFAC), 210 Century Building, 36 South Pennsylvania Street, Indianapolis, IN 46204, (317) 633-4210.

Laboratory for Manufacturing and Productivity (LMP), MIT 35-234, 77 Massachusetts Avenue, Cambridge, MA 02139, (617) 253-2234.

Laser Center, IIT Research Institute, 10 West 35th Street, Chicago, IL 60616, (312) 567-4228.

Little People's Productivity Center, 2580 Grand Avenue, Baldwin, NY 11510, (516) 623-6295.

Machinability Data Center (MDC), Metcut Research Associates, Inc., 3980 Rosslyn Drive, Cincinnati, OH 45209, (513) 271-9510.

Management of Advanced Automation Technology (MAAT) WPI, Washburn Building, Room 212, Worcester, MA 01609.

Manufacturing Engineering Applications Centers, Worcester Polytechnic Institute, Washburn Laboratories, Room 307, Worcester, MA 01609, (617) 793-5335.

Manufacturing Productivity Center (MPC), ITT Research Institute, 10 West 35th Street, Chicago, IL 60616, (312) 567-4800.

Manufacturing Systems Engineering (MSE), University of Wisconsin—Madison, 1513 University Avenue, Madison, WI 53706, (608) 262-0921.

Masters Degree in Manufacturing, Department of Mechanical Engineering, Pittsburgh, PA 15213, (412) 268-2501.

Material Handling Research Center, Georgia Institute of Technology, 765 Ferst N.W., Atlanta, GA 30332-0206.

Purdue Laboratory for Applied Industrial Control (PLAIC), Purdue University, A.A. Potter Engineering Center, Room 334, West Lafayette, IN 47907, (317) 494-7434.

Robotics Research Center, Wales Hall, University of Rhode Island, Kingston, RI 02881-0805, (401) 792-2531.

Stanford Institute for Manufacturing and Automation (SIMA) School of Engineering, Stanford University, Stanford, CA 94305-4028, (415) 723-9038.

GLOSSARY

GENERAL BUSINESS TERMS*

A

Account. A record of a business transaction or "deal." When you buy something on credit, the company you are dealing with sets up an "account," which means a record of what you buy and the amount you pay. You will do the same thing with any customers to whom you extend credit. At the bank, you will also have an account, a record of what you deposit and withdraw.

Accountant. One who is skilled at keeping business records. The term "accountant" usually refers to a highly trained professional rather than to one who keeps books. An accountant knows how

---

* These terms are used in the SBA Prospective Small Business Owners Workshop script, "Keys to Business Success." The simple definition given for each term is not intended to be the only or complete definition but rather to clarify the term in the context of the Workshop presentation.

221

to set up the books needed to operate a business, and he or she can help a business owner understand what the business records mean.

Accounts receivable. A record of what is owed to you. All of the credit accounts—what each customer owes you taken together—are your "accounts receivable." Even though you don't have the money in hand, money that is owed to you is an asset, like property you own. You have to know your accounts receivable in order to know what your business is worth at any time. Of course, your accounts receivable must be collected to become a real asset.

Analysis. The breaking down of an idea or a problem into its parts. In business you must "analyze" a problem before you can decide on the best solution. Let's say your problem is some item that isn't selling well. You make a list of things that might be wrong and ask questions like, is the price right? What have customers said about the item? Etc. An analysis includes gathering facts that might help explain the problem and indicate its solution.

Appraisal. An estimated value set after inspection of a business or property. It is used as a starting point for negotiations in borrowing funds, severing a partnership, defending a lawsuit, or making an insurance settlement.

Articles of incorporation. A legal document that sets forth the purposes and regulations of a corporation. These papers must be approved by the appropriate state office before a corporation legally exists and can do business. Each state has different requirements and the procedures are complicated, so it is usually necessary to hire a lawyer specializing in corporate law for this process.

Asset. Anything of worth that is owned. Your personal assets (not counting your abilities) are the money you have in your pocket or in the bank, whatever is owed to you, any securities and property you own, your furniture and appliances, and all the miscellaneous things that you personally own. The assets of a business are just the same: money in the bank, accounts receivable, securities held in the name of the business, real estate, equipment fixtures, merchandise, supplies, and all the real things of value that the business owns.

B

Bad debt. Money owed to you that you can't collect. The risk of "bad debts" is why a business should carefully consider giving credit and lending money. When it is apparent that an account is not collectible, that account should not be kept on the books as an asset. An accountant can advise when and how to enter such accounts as bad debts.

Balance. As a noun, the amount of money remaining in a bank account after accounting for all transactions (deposits and withdrawals). Also, the amount of money you owe a creditor, or a customer owes. As a verb, when the amounts of money in a positive (credit) account and a negative (debit) account are made equal. Think of an account as an old-fashioned set of scales. When there is nothing on either side, they are "balanced." When credit is extended, it is like putting an amount of money on one side—the weight makes that basket go down. When money is paid on the account it is like putting weight on the opposite side. When enough money is paid back, the scales will equal or balance again.

Balance sheet. An important business record that shows what a business owns and owes at any one time. A "balance sheet" lists business assets and their present value on one side of a ledger and liabilities on the other. The liabilities include the net worth of the business, which the business "owes" the owner. If the balance sheet has been figured correctly, it must balance.

Business Development Corporation (BDC). A business financing agency, usually made up of the financial institutions in an area or state, and organized for assisting industrial concerns that are not able to obtain such assistance through normal channels. The risk is spread among various members of the BDC, and interest rates may vary somewhat from those charged by member institutions.

Business venture. A financial risk taken in a commercial enterprise. Successful businesspeople have learned that they can control the risk by practicing good management and getting advice from bankers, accountants, lawyers, and business associates.

C

Capital. Available money to invest or the total accumulated assets you can make available for starting a business and for living on while the business is in the early stages. If you are successful, the business will accumulate "capital" in the form of property, goods, and money (including securities).

Capital requirement. A list (or schedule) of expenses that must be met to establish a business—i.e., how much capital must be invested to start the business and keep it operating. One item of importance that is often forgotten is the amount of money that will be needed for living expenses until the business starts earning a profit.

Cash. Currency—hard money, bills, and negotiable securities (like checks)—in your cash drawer or readily available. The money you can draw on demand—your bank accounts or savings accounts—also represents "cash." You must have it to keep a business going, and even a very successful business can run out, particularly as the business is growing. So good managers plan ahead on their needs for cash.

Cash receipts. The money received by a business from customers. "Cash receipts" are to a business what food and water are to living things. A business can survive just so long on its stored-up capital. Businesspeople preserve their capital as much as possible and try to have a regular, sufficient flow of cash.

Certified Development Corporation (SBA 503 Program). A local or statewide corporation or authority that packages SBA, bank, state, and private money into a financial assistance package for existing business capital improvement (both for profit and nonprofit concerns). Each state has at least one CDC. The SBA holds the second lien on its maximum share of 40 percent involvement; this is called the "503 Program."

Certified lenders. Banks that participate in the SBA's guaranteed loan program, have a good track record with the SBA, and agree to certain conditions set forth by the SBA. In return, the SBA agrees to process any guaranteed loan application within three business days. District offices of the SBA can provide lists of certified banks in their areas.

Chain of command. The proper lines of authority among the head of an organization, its manager, supervisors, and workers. In every well-organized business, there should be a line of authority that everyone understands. Sometimes a "chain-of-command" graph is useful in making this clear. A good manager will make sure employees understand the order of authority and the method of communicating with management.

Contract. A legally binding agreement regarding mutual responsibilities between two or more parties. In business law, a "contract" exists whenever there has been a meeting of minds—whether or not the contract is written. However, contracts are usually made in written form and should never be taken lightly. Any business contract should be examined by a qualified lawyer. It should also be read thoroughly by the parties and signed only after its meaning is clearly understood. Note that many sales forms are binding contracts and should not be signed unless the terms of the agreement are clearly understood.

Controllable expenses. Costs of doing business that can be restrained, meaning postponed or spread out over a period of time. For example, depreciation on equipment is a "controllable expense" in that it isn't required. A businessperson can put off obtaining new equipment until the business can support the purchase and its depreciation.

Corporation. A business structure, created by a state charter, comprising a group of individuals or objects treated by the law as an individual. Thus, a corporation is an artificial personage; acting through its officers, it can do business as a separate entity the way individuals can in a sole proprietorship or a partnership. Unlike the case with other types of ownership, a corporation may be owned by a number of persons, who hold shares.

Cosigners. Joint signers of a loan agreement, pledging to meet the obligations in case of default. When you ask someone to "cosign" a note, you are asking that person to share a debt with you and guarantee that the loan will be paid back. The lender can take legal action against cosigners' property if they refuse to pay. This arrangement should not be entered into lightly by either borrowers or cosigners.

D

Debit. Debts recorded. Bookkeeping deals with "credits" and "debits" in putting down the additions and subtractions of business capital; debits are the minus or negative entries in the books— the money that is taken out of a particular account. Usually, books are set up so that debits are recorded in the left-hand column of an account.

Debt. That which is owed. If you borrow money, buy something on credit, or receive more money on an account than is owed, you have a "debt"—an obligation to pay back whatever amount is involved. Going into debt was once considered a sin, but it can be useful and is often a necessary way of doing business. A debt is bad business when it is larger than the ability of the borrower to repay.

Default. Failure to pay a debt or meet an obligation. Any debt is a trust, and failure to pay it is a violation of a serious kind. To "default" is to demonstrate that you are untrustworthy and do possibly irreparable damage to your reputation. In business such a poor reputation can, and probably will, restrict your credit and cost you valuable creditors and business friends; ultimately, it may cost you your business.

Depreciation. A decrease in value through age, wear, or deterioration. It is said that an automobile "depreciates" as soon as it is driven off the lot, it immediately becomes a "used" car and is worth something less to the owner than when it was brand new. In the same way, all the equipment you buy for a business begins to depreciate immediately and is worth increasingly less as it continues to be used. Depreciation is a normal expense of doing business, but it is a real expense that must be taken into account. When a new piece of equipment is purchased, it is set up as an item in a "depreciation account" whereby it can be expensed over a period of time. There are regulations governing the manner and periods of time that may be used for depreciation, in that the rate of depreciation affects a business's taxable income.

Direct loans. Financial assistance provided through the lending of federal monies for a specific period of time, with a reasonable expectation of repayment. Such loans may or may not require the payment of interest.

Disaster loans. Various kinds of physical and economic assistance available to individuals and businesses who have suffered losses due to natural disaster. This is the only SBA loan program available for residential purposes.

E

Economics. The management of financial resources, whether of nation, city, and business or of an individual. A small-business owner does well to have a basic understanding of "economics" because it is such an important matter in the conduct of business.

Embezzle. To steal or take by fraud another's property for one's own use. One of the great perils of doing business is that seemingly trustworthy people sometimes are moved to steal from their employers and associates. Many businesses have been unable to survive the effects of such acts. There are three ways to protect a business against "embezzlement": careful selection of those people who are the best risks, business procedures that make the practice difficult, and insurance or bonding against any loss that may occur.

Enterprise. A business firm or a business undertaking. In a general sense, "enterprise" refers to any hard, dangerous, or important project, which makes the term apt for business, because a successful business has all these attributes.

Entrepreneur. A person who organizes and manages a business. This is a French word that has been accepted into the English language. Its popularity probably has something to do with its grand sound which befits anyone who has the initiative to create and run a business.

Equity capital. Venture money. In order to go into business you will certainly have to lay it on the line. You put up savings or property when you go into business in hopes of getting a good return. Unfortunately, some people who have worked hard and protected their savings magnificiently still make foolish investments. It is very important to consider carefully before investing in your own business and to take all the steps you can to protect your "equity capital."

F

Factor. Generally, something that contributes to a result; in business, a finance company specializing in short-term, high-risk loans (usually at high interest rates). The first meaning has to do with "facts" or "factual things" that are a part of any subject. When we speak of the "factors" involved in borrowing money, we mean the facts that the banker or loan officer must know in order to approve a loan. The second meaning of "factor" is specific to the finance business. Factors who lend money to a high-risk enterprise usually require collateral and may exercise control of the enterprise.

Financial statement. A record of total assets and liabilities. Knowing what you or your business is worth is rather important. It's a way to find out whether you are advancing or retreating in the conduct of your affairs, and, as such, is an aid to making business decisions. In a sense, the financial statement is the certificate of success or failure. In order to borrow any appreciable amount of money, the lender will require an accurate financial statement.

Financing. Obtaining money resources. Businesses usually have to obtain financing at some time—either to get started or to expand operations (hopefully not just to stay in business). The time to set up relationships with those who might provide financing is before you need the money. Maybe you won't ever need financing, but that would be most unusual, so you would be well advised to lay the groundwork early.

Fixed expenses. Costs that don't vary from one period to the next—i.e., that are not affected by the volume of business. Rent, for example, must be paid whether or not any business is conducted. "Fixed expenses" are the basic costs that a businessperson has each month.

Franchise. A right or privilege to deal in a certain line or brand of goods and services. A franchising company (franchisor) is in the business of "selling" businesses or brands to small entrepreneurs (franchisees). Usually, the franchisor and the franchisee enter into a binding contract providing that the franchisor will supply the product, materials, and a certain amount of know-how, and the franchisee will handle the product exclusively and run the business according to certain standards prescribed by the franchisor. Such a relationship may be mutually advantageous, but it is a long-term arrangement that should be examined carefully before being accepted.

Functional. Relating to a function or a characteristic action. In a general sense, the term is used to describe an object that is useful rather than ornamental. In business, a "functional" organization means an organization structured around the activities of the business, in contrast with the more formal "line management" organization. A functional organization has specialists who serve as managers rather than managers who only manage and are not specialists.

G

Gross. The whole amount of income, before deductions and expenses. One has to learn early the difference between "gross" and "net" figures, for many new businesspeople get fooled by the gross figures. These may show a business making a substantial "gross" profit, but by the time all the expenses are deducted, the "net" or real profit is small. Another meaning of "gross" is "very wrong," and that's exactly how it is if a businessperson confuses gross with net.

Guaranteed/insured loans. Loan programs in which the federal government makes an arrangement to indemnify lenders against part or all of any defaults by those responsible for repayment of the loans.

I

Income. Money coming in. "Income" means essentially the same for a business as for an individual. It is all the money received before anything is taken out. See "gross."

Incubators. Facilities for encouraging entrepreneurship by housing in one place a number of fledgling enterprises that share an array of services. These shared services may include meeting areas, secretarial services, accounting, research library, on-site financial and management counseling, and computer word-processing facilities. "Incubators" facilitate new business formation and growth, particularly for high technology firms.

Industrial Development Authority. The financial arm of a state or other political subdivision established for supporting economic development in an area. This is usually done through loans to nonprofit organizations, which in turn provide facilities for manufacturing and other industrial operations.

Industry Ratio. The average percentage of income spent by firms in the same industry on various cost items. These "industry ratio" figures are very important guidelines for a business. The point is not that a businessperson ought to adhere rigidly to the industry averages, but by comparing costs with what similar businesses spend, he or she can look for areas that seem to be out of line. If for example, a business's expenditures are only half of the industry ratio, the business owner would do well to consider additional advertising.

Interest. The cost of borrowing money. Banks and loan companies are businesses like any others. They have to receive a profitable income or they can't attract money, expand, and provide the services that banks must provide. Of course, any "interest" or price you pay comes right off the top of your income and is subtracted from your profit. Shop for a good interest rate as you would for anything you buy.

Inventory. A list of present or current material assets. If you are in a retail business, the stock you have on the shelves is "inventory," but so are your available supplies, goods received or stored, and any expendable items on hand. As a regular part of the book-keeping process, inventory must be counted periodically because it is needed to figure what the business is worth.

Invest. Lay out money for any venture from which a profit is expected. One way to evaluate whether investing in a business is worthwhile is to consider what you would make by putting that money into a low-risk investment. The prospects should be for a much greater return if money is risked in a business.

L

Labor Surplus Areas. Places that are designated as "labor surplus" have high unemployment. This information is requested on pro-curement bid sheets, and firms bidding for jobs are given extra points.

Lease. A long-term rental agreement. A "lease" arrangement is mutually advantageous to both the lessor owner and the lessee (renter). The agreement assures the landlord that the property will be rented, and assures the renter that the business property will not be taken out from under the business. It is a good idea to have a lease option for extending the rental period, but be careful. Businesses often find that they did not plan on sufficient space and are bound by a lease they cannot get out of.

Liability. That which is owed. This is one of the business words that have more than one application and can be confusing. There is "liability" insurance, which is insurance to cover any claims that are brought against the policy holder (see below). But the term "liabilities" usually refers to the obligations of the business as opposed to its assets. Of course, the business also has a liability toward its owner, so with the list of what the business owes there is always an ownership liability, which is the difference between what a business owns and what it owes to those other than the owners.

Liability insurance. Protection a business carries to cover the possibility of loss from lawsuits in the event the business or its agents are found to be at fault if an accident occurs. It protects the business investment.

Limited partnership. A legal arrangement in which some owners are allowed to assume responsibility only up to the amount invested. The idea in a "limited partnership" is that investors may put up money for a business venture without being directly involved in its operation and so are not held responsible for the debts of the other partners beyond the possible loss of the money they have invested.

Line position. A place of authority in a "line" organization. Having a "line position" means being responsible only to the person directly above you in the organization.

Liquidate. To settle a debt or to convert to cash. This word literally means "to do away with"; in a business sense, "liquidate" means to do away with a debt by paying it, or to do away with material assets by selling them and thus turning them into cash.

Loan. Money borrowed with an interest charge.

Local development corporation. An organization, usually made up of local citizens, whose aim is to improve the economy of the area by inducing business and industry to locate there. A "local development corporation" usually has financing capabilities.

M

Management. The art of conducting and supervising a business. It isn't enough just to invest money in a business; someone—a manager—must nurture, protect, and help the business along to success. Another way to look at it is that "management" is the exercise of judgment in business affairs.

Marketing. All the functions involved in buying and selling. It is often said about business that nothing happens until somebody sells something, so "marketing" is really the heart of a business operation. Marketing includes advertising, sales promotion, and even public relations.

Merchandise. Goods bought and sold in a business. "Merchandise" or stock is a part of inventory. In usage, merchandise has come to mean anything movable that can be sold or traded.

Minority businesses. The Small Business Administration defines minorities as those who are "socially or economically disadvantaged." Social disadvantage has to do with membership in one of several different racial or ethnic categories as defined by regulation (or on a case-by-case basis for others who feel they are socially disadvantaged, like the physically handicapped). Groups that are considered to be socially disadvantaged include Black Americans, Hispanic Americans, Native Americans (American Indians, Eskimos, Aleuts, and Native Hawaiians), Asian Pacific Americans (people originating in Japan, China, the Philippines, Vietnam, Korea, Samoa, Guam, U.S. Trust Territory of the Pacific Islands, Northern Mariana Islands, Laos, Cambodia, and Taiwan), and Subcontinent Asian Americans. Economic disadvantage has to do with the barriers that social disadvantage has placed in the way of an individual's employment and participation in business. In most cases, being a woman does not by itself qualify a person for minority status.

Minority Enterprise Small Business Investment Company (MESBIC). MESBICs are licensed by the SBA as federally funded, private venture capital funds. They are comparable to SBICs, except that the MESBICs are targeted toward socially or economically disadvantaged individuals.

Motivation. Strong influence or incentive. "Motivation" is the force that moves a person to do whatever he or she does. It may be something that the person is not even aware of, and a whole field of business psychology has grown up around motivation research—the study of why people buy things, including hidden reasons.

N

Net. What is left after deducting all charges. See "gross."

Nonrecurring. One time, not repeating. "Nonrecurring" expenses, like those involved in starting a business, only have to be paid once and will not occur again.

O

Objective. A goal toward which effort is directed; something to accomplish. Note that "objective" also means "realistic"; we could say that "objectives" are aims set to produce some realistic result.

Obsolescence. Decline in value because of replacement by newer or better things. People have a way of wanting whatever is the latest style or development, so a businessperson will do well to guard against "obsolescence" and not overstock items that tend to change style.

Office of Small and Disadvantaged Business Utilization (OSDBU). Each agency of the federal government has an office located in Washington that is a watchdog over it—assuring that the agency complies with federal regulations to purchase a certain percentage of products and services from small and minority-owned-and-operated businesses. If small businesses can't get help from one of these, they can contact the OSDBU in Washington.

Operating costs. Expenditures arising out of current business activities. Your "operating costs" for any period of time are simply what it costs you to do business—the salaries and charges for electricity, rental, deliveries, etc., that were involved in performing the business dealings.

Operating organization. The management structure as opposed to legal structure of a firm.

Operating ratios. The relationship among costs arising from business activities, such as the percentage of costs that went for rent. How does that compare with other businesses like yours? These are facts that a business needs to operate efficiently and not waste resources.

Organize. To put in order. A good manager can make order out of just about anything—a work force, a payment schedule, or a merchandise display plan. There is a logic to every task, and using that logic is what it means to "organize."

Owner-manager. One who operates his or her own business. One of the greatest assets an "owner-manager" has is flexibility in meeting problems. There is no need to call a committee together or consult the board of directors to take action. Being a good owner-manager is one of the most satisfying of endeavors.

Ownership organization. The legal as opposed to management structure of a business. How a business is organized legally depends upon how it is owned. If one person owns it it's usually a proprietorship; if several people own it jointly as owner-managers, it's a partnership (unless incorporated). If many people own a business, it almost certainly is some form of a corporation.

P

Partnership. A legal business relationship in which individuals share responsibilities, resources, and profits. Partnerships are built on mutual trust, but trust should be backed up with a firm agreement in writing.

Payable. Ready to be paid. One of the standard accounts kept by the bookkeeper is "accounts payable." This is simply a list of bills that are current and due to be paid.

Pay on demand. An order to comply with an obligation. Contracts are often written with a "pay-on-demand" clause, which means the debtor must pay the balance when asked, even if the terms of the contract agreement have been met.

Personnel. Collective term for all people in the employ of a business. As a small business grows, it will need "personnel" to handle the expansion of the business and carry out its work.

Pledge. To bind by a promise; to give possession of something of value as security for a loan. There has to be a great deal of trust between parties doing business—indeed, it seems doubtful that business could proceed without it, for it is the basis for all credit transactions, most business agreements, and the general conduct of commerce. For the most part, we accept the first kind of "pledge" from other people, and usually they keep their promises. However, the second kind of "pledge" is sometimes called for, particularly when sizable amounts of money are involved, and is a more formal arrangement. The borrowing party then pledges (usually in writing) to give possession of some capital assets if he or she is unable to meet the terms of the obligation.

Post. To enter an account in the books.

Pricing. Setting a value upon something. How well a small businessperson handles "pricing" may determine if there is a profit and how much. An operation as important as pricing should not be left to "what the traffic will bear" or "what the other outfits are charging." It is far better to establish prices scientifically by figuring out all the costs involved and adding a fair profit—*then* comparing your prices with the market.

Principal. Property or capital assets as opposed to income; also, one who is directly concerned in a business enterprise. If you consider that the word means "the first in importance"—whether referring to people or capital assets—the usage becomes clearer. The money you invest in a business is the first in importance— "principal." And if you are investing money and effort in business you are a "principal."

Procurement assistance. A kind of contract from the Government offering special opportunities to qualifying businesses. Small businesses should be particularly interested in two types of "procurement": (1) small-business set-asides, which are required by law to be on all contracts under $10,000, or a certain percentage of an agency's total procurement expenditure; and (2) the SBA 8(a) program, in which small and minority-owned-and-operated businesses can negotiate on special contracts.

Profit. Financial gain—return over expenditures, or, most simply put, what you've got left after paying for everything. Hopefully, the "profit" represents a good return on the investment in a business, plus reward payment for good management; but never take profit for granted—it can be disappointing.

Profit & loss statement. A list of the total amount of sales less expenses and costs, to show the amount of "profit or loss" for doing business. It is sometimes called an "income statement."

Profit margin. An allowance above expenditures made in setting a price. A businessperson plans for profits by building them into prices (see "pricing").

Prompt pay. A ruling that if federal government agencies do not pay invoices for goods and services within 45 days of billing, they have to pay interest to the vendor on any amount overdue.

Proprietorship. Exclusive ownership. A "proprietor" is one who owns a business, and a business owned by one person is called a "proprietorship."

R

Ratio. The relationship of one thing to another expressed as numbers or degrees. For example, we say that a greengrocer has a 10 to 1 loss ratio on lettuce, which is a short way of saying that for every 10 heads of lettuce he or she buys, the grocer loses one head that either doesn't sell or spoils before it can be sold and has to be thrown away. "Ratios" of this kind are established by keeping figures over a period of time. The ratio here is figured by dividing the number lost into the number sold.

Receivable. Unpaid and ready for payment. See "accounts receivable." In accounting, a "receivable"—money that is owed to you—is an asset; it is listed as a current asset in the balance sheet.

Regulations. Rules of law. It is accepted in our system of government that the state has the obligation to protect citizens, so the government has established laws to prevent injury. Some of these have to do with business practices and must be followed to avoid penalties. Of course, many such regulations benefit the small businessperson.

Reserve. That which is held back and stored for future use or in case of emergency. The success or failure of many young businesses depends upon their ability to weather a financial crisis. There should be something in "reserve" to meet an emergency.

Retail. Selling in small quantities directly to the consumer, in contrast with selling in large quantities to dealers for resale, which is a "wholesale" activity. There is some confusion brought about by advertising that says "discount," "cut-rate," or "wholesale prices," but these operations are really "retail" as long as they are selling in small amounts to the general public.

S

SCORE/ACE. The Service Corps of Retired Executives and the Active Corps of Executives, a combined volunteer management assistance program of the SBA. SCORE and ACE volunteers provide one-on-one counseling free of charge and offer workshops and seminars for a small fee.

Secured loans. A loan that is protected or guaranteed. To "secure" means to make an object safe, so a "secured loan" is one that is made safe by something of value put up as collateral.

Service business. A retail business that deals in activities for the benefit of others. If you go to a doctor or lawyer, he or she will send you a bill marked "for services rendered." Other examples are a laundry, an auto repair shop, a beauty salon, etc.

Share. One of the equal parts into which the worth of a corporation is divided for sale. Thus, "share" represents a part ownership in a corporation. The more shares one holds, the more ownership one has.

Site. A plot of ground set aside for a particular use. The business "site" may or may not be owned by the business, and it is often better to rent a "site" when getting started.

Small Business Investment Corporation (SBIC). Federally funded, private venture capital firms licensed by the SBA. Money is available to small businesses under a variety of agreements. This money is usually, but not always, expansion capital for new, risky, or high-tech firms.

Stabilizing. Becoming less subject to ups and downs. Like a ship on the ocean, a business may run into a "rough sea" of changing conditions. Successful businesspeople look for "stabilizing" methods to smooth out these conditions—whether by diversifying into products that are more "stable," by eliminating the factors that cause the fluctuations, or by operating on a level that minimizes the effects of the fluctuations.

Stock. An ownership share in a corporation (another name for share); also, accumulated merchandise, a merchant's wares. Putting merchandise out for display is called "stocking the shelves."

Surety bond. A guarantee of reimbursement to an individual, company, or the government if a firm fails to complete a contract. The SBA backs "surety bonds" in a program much like its guaranteed loan program.

T

Trade credit. Permission to buy from suppliers on an open account. When you buy business supplies on credit, you are really borrowing from the supplier—you have the loan of whatever he or she is selling you until it is paid for. Suppliers usually extend this service for a period of time (often 20 to 30 days) without charging interest, but it is not uncommon to charge interest sooner if the amount is large and the time to repay is extended. "Trade credit" is useful to small businesspeople, who should keep their reputations bright so they may continue the privilege.

Transfer. To move from one place to another or from one person to another. One of the main services of banks is to provide the efficient "transfer" of funds. The practice of using checks is to accomplish the transfer of money without the need for moving the money physically.

Tangible. Real. The literal meaning is "can be touched," but the business meaning refers to something that can be seen and evaluated. "Tangible" assets are those that have a real value and can be converted, if necessary, into cash. The "intangible" assets of a business are attributes that may be of value but can't be measured or objectively evaluated—for example, the good will that a business has built up.

Tax number. A number assigned by a state revenue department that enables a business to buy goods wholesale without paying the sales tax.

V

Venture capital. Money used to support new or unusual undertakings; equity, risk, or speculative investment capital. This funding is provided to new or existing firms that exhibit above-average growth. See "business venture."

Volume. An amount of quantity. The "volume" of a business is the total it sells over a period of time.

W

Wholesale. Selling for resale. See "retail."

TERMS OF SALE (TERMS OF PAYMENT)

Date of invoice. All terms originate from date of invoice. The date cannot be prior to day of shipment. Note: Terms may expire prior to receipt of goods.

Dated, or As of. Terms do not begin with the date of the invoice but at a later specified date. If an invoice is "dated" May 1 and reads "2% 10 days net 30 plus 30 days," the terms become effective June 1. If the invoice says "2% 10 days net 30 as of April," terms of payment begin April 1.

Discount. Usually expressed as a percentage of the net. Discounts cannot be taken on taxes or freight shown separately on invoices.

E.O.M. End of month. The buyer can wait until the end of the month during which purchases are made before credit terms (or discount terms) become effective. Example: The buyer received an invoice dated June 20; terms of payment do not begin until July 1.

Net. No discount; bottom figure on invoice including tax. The "net" is usually accompanied by terms of when due—i.e., "on receipt of invoice," "10 days," "30 days," "10th Prox.,"etc. If date terms are shown, the amount is due on receipt of invoice and no discount is allowed.

Prox. Abbreviation for "proximo," which means "next following."

2% 10th Prox, Net 30th Prox. If an invoice is dated on or before the 25th, a discount of 2% is allowed if the bill is paid by the following 10th. Otherwise, the net is due July 30th. If an invoice is dated after the 25th, then the 2% discount is allowed by the 10th of the second month and the net is due by the 30th of the second month.

TERMS FOR INTERNATIONAL TRADE

A

Advising bank. A bank operating in the exporter's country that handles letters of credit for a foreign bank by notifying the exporter that the credit has been opened in his or her favor. The advising bank fully informs the exporter of the conditions of the letter of credit without necessarily bearing responsibility for payment.

Arbitrage. The process of buying foreign exchange, stocks, bonds, and other commodities in one market and immediately selling them in another market at higher prices.

B

Barter. Trade in which merchandise is exchanged directly for other merchandise without the use of money. Barter is an important means of trade with countries using currency that is not readily convertible.

C

Collection paper. Any document (commercial invoice, bill of lading, etc.) submitted to a buyer for the purpose of receiving payment for a shipment.

Commercial attaché. The commerce expert on the diplomatic staff of a country's embassy or large consulate.

Consular declaration. A formal statement, made to the consul of a foreign country, describing goods to be shipped.

Consular invoice. A document, required by some foreign countries, describing a shipment of goods and showing information such as the names of the consignor and consignee and the value of the shipment.

Convertible currency. A currency that can be bought and sold for other currencies at will.

Correspondent bank. A bank that, in its own country, handles the business of a foreign bank.

Countertrade. The sale of goods or services that are paid for in whole or in part by the transfer of goods or services from a foreign country. See "barter."

Customhouse broker. An individual or firm licensed to enter and clear goods through customs.

Customs. The authorities designated to collect duties levied by a country on imports and exports. The term also applies to the procedures involved in such collection.

D

Destination control statement. Any of various statements the U.S. Government requires to be displayed on export shipments that specify the destinations authorized for shipment.

Drawback. Refund of duty related to articles manufactured or produced in the United States for export with the use of imported components or raw materials. Manufacturers are entitled to a refund of up to 99 percent of the duty charged on the imported components.

E

Exchange permit. A permit sometimes required by the importer's government enabling the importer to convert his or her own country's currency into foreign currency with which to pay a seller in another country.

Exchange rate. The price of one currency in terms of another— i.e., the number of units of one currency that may be exchanged for one unit of another currency.

Export broker. An individual or firm that brings together buyers and sellers for a fee but does not take part in the actual sales transactions.

Export commission house. An organization that acts as a purchasing agent for foreign buyers, for a commission.

Export license. A government document that permits the licensee to engage in the export of designated goods to certain destinations. See "general export license" and "validated export license."

Export management company. A private firm that serves as the export department for several manufacturers. It solicits and transacts export business on behalf of its clients in return for a commission, salary, or retainer plus commission.

Export trading company. A firm similar to an export management company, but with a broader range of services, including the taking of title to goods.

F

Foreign sales agent. An individual or firm that serves as the foreign representative of a domestic supplier and seeks sales abroad for the supplier.

Free port. An area such as a port city into which merchandise may be moved without payment of duties.

Free trade zone. A port designated by the government of a country for duty-free entry of any nonprohibited goods. Merchandise may be stored, displayed, used for manufacturing, etc., within the zone and reexported without duties being paid. Duties are imposed on the merchandise (or items manufactured from the merchandise) only when the goods pass from the zone into an area of the country subject to the customs authority.

G

General Agreement on Tariffs and Trade (GATT). A multilateral treaty intended to help reduce trade barriers between the signatory countries and to promote trade through tariff concessions.

General export license. Any of various export licenses covering commodities for which "validated export licenses" are not required. No formal application or written authorization is needed to ship goods under a "general export license."

L

Letter of credit (L/C). A document, consisting of instructions by a buyer of goods, that is issued by a bank to the seller, who is authorized to draw a specific sum of money under certain conditions (i.e., the receipt by the bank of certain documents within a given time). An "irrevocable L/C" provides a guarantee by the issuing bank in the event that all terms and conditions are met by the buyer (or drawee). A "revocable L/C" can be canceled or altered by the drawee after it has been issued by drawee's bank. A "confirmed L/C" is one that is issued by a foreign bank and validated or guaranteed by a U.S. bank for a U.S. exporter in the case of default by the foreign buyer or bank.

P

Private Export Funding Corporation (PEFCO). Lends to foreign buyers to finance exports from the United States.

Purchasing agent. An agent who purchases goods in his or her own country on behalf of foreign importers, such as government agencies and large private concerns.

Q

Quota. The quantity of goods of a specific kind that a country permits to be imported without restriction or imposition of additional duties.

S

Schedule B. Refers to Schedule B Statistical Classification of Domestic and Foreign Commodities Exported from the United States. All commodities exported from the United States must be assigned a seven-digit Schedule B number.

Shipper's export declaration. A form required by the U.S. Treasury Department for all export shipments. It is prepared by a shipper and indicates the value, weight, destination, and other basic information about the shipment.

V

Validated export license. A document issued by the U.S. Government authorizing the export of commodities, covering a specific transaction or time period in which the exporting is to take place.

INDEX

INDEX

INDEX